MISFIT

MISFIT

MISTER JOHN

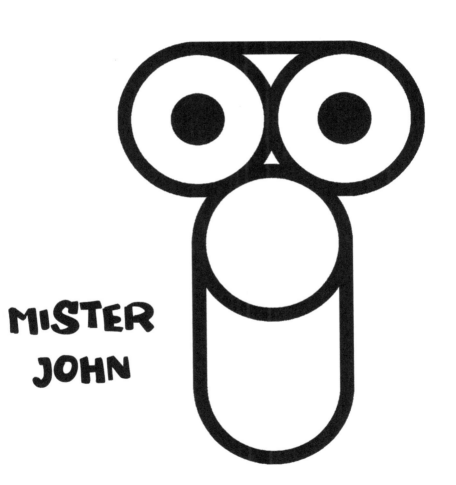

Copyright © 2024 Mister John

All rights reserved.

In accordance with the U.S. Copyright Act of 1976, the scanning, uploading, and electronic sharing of any part of this book without the author's permission constitutes unlawful piracy and theft of the author's intellectual property. If you would like to use material from this book (other than for review purposes), you must obtain prior written permission by contacting the author at: misterjohn@me.com

Thank you for supporting the author's rights.

Some names, locations, and dates may have been changed for privacy.

First Edition
ISBN: 979-8-9900202-4-5

Cover Graphic © John Curran
Cover Design by John Curran
Author photograph © Sue L. Harrington

Author website: misterjohn.me

Fonts:
Adobe Garamond Pro by Robert Slimbach
Bobby Donut by Wahyu Eka Prasetya

YAK Publishing
Publisher website: yakpublishing.com

DEDICATION

*

TO SUE
WHO KNEW
WHAT I SHOULD DO

*

TABLE OF CONTENTS

STORY	TITLE	PAGE
001	FIRST 14 HOURS	1
002	LAST FIRST DATE	9
003	527 CENTRE STREET	14
004	THOSE WITH ILLINOIS PLATES	22
005	BOY!	27
006	NICE HAT	34
007	DUBAI TO HAIDA GWAII	38
008	OUR BOXES WERE GETTING TICKED	43
009	IT WAS A DARK AND STORMY NIGHT	48
010	OLD LADY ANTHONY	54
011	JOHNNY GOT BACK	58
012	A SENSE OF HUMOR	66
013	YOU KICK ANY WAY YOU WANT	72
014	LOSE YOUR ASS-WIPING MIND	79
015	MENS NOT ALLOWED	86
016	417 1/2 McDONOUGH STREET	89
017	WINNER WINNER CHICKEN DINNER	97
018	WE'RE CHICKENS	103
019	YOU'RE A FATHER!	107
020	SNOWBALL FIGHT	114
021	THE BUICK'S LAST RIDE	119
022	I'LL NEVER FORGET MY FIRST	124
023	QUEPASACONSUBASURA	130
024	NUMBERS FIRST	133
025	GO CALL YOUR MOTHER	136
026	THE EMPTY DESK	143
027	OUTSIDE THE BOX	147
028	T.A.I.W.	153
029	WHO WAS THE NOVELTY	158
030	KEVIN BACON LOOKS JUST LIKE YOU	162
031	I'VE BEEN TO ELVIS' HOUSE	166
032	MY MOTHER GETS AROUND	171
033	I KNOW THERE BEFORE I AM	176
034	STORY NIGHT	180
035	THE THINGS I REMEMBER	185
036	MISFIT	192

PREFACE
JUST A PAGE

Mired in a soul-crushing stretch at the University of Wisconsin-Milwaukee, one of my favorite people, Brenda, suggested I drop out of school and take up writing as a career. Even though I think she was joking, I considered her suggestion, not seeing a rewarding future resulting from either of my majors - architecture and economics.

While I continued my studies, I never forgot her words, heeding them some twenty years after I "dropped out" of Dubai Women's College, where I'd been teaching Emirati women... computers and math. Retiring at 44, I moved - with another of my favorite people, a Canadian librarian, Sue, who would become my wife - to a property off a dead-end dirt road on a mountainside near Vilcabamba, Ecuador.

After spending a year deciding how to renovate our new home and then another doing but not quite finishing it, the previous owner of the property, Lee, helped get my writing career started, linking me with his employer, a company catering to expatriates and expat wannabes. Apparently, he liked what he read in my half of the emails we exchanged before and after we purchased his property.

Brenda based her suggestion on the writing of mine she'd read or heard me read as far back as middle school. Then there were the letters I wrote her when people sent letters - stamps, envelopes, and a postal service required. Sitting in my dorm room at the keyboard of Ma's old Smith Corona electric typewriter, I'd tap out whatever came to mind, often with no capitalization or punctuation, to give my fingers a chance to keep up. They seldom could.

Even though my words have always flowed freely, I don't think of myself so much as a writer as a transcriber for the voices inside my head, the hard part making sense of them all. Both blessed and cursed with a memory that rarely forgets, those voices narrate every thread of my life, why what I write, or say, on occasion causes Sue to shake her head, "Where'd that come from?" Why, five years after my writing career began, she encouraged me to stop writing for others and write for myself.

"Give your voices a voice, and they'll quiet down."

I thought it wise to listen to Sue - happy wife, happy life - and started transcribing those voices. Despite the cacophony from the real-life Fisher-Price See 'n Say® The Farmer Says® going on around (and sometimes in) our home, along with life's many distractions, my other projects, my photography, and Sue's constant interruptions, I've written more since her suggestion than I ever have.

Even when I was in sixth grade and my English teacher, Mrs. Winkler, with silver-colored glasses matching the hair bee-hived high upon her head, assigned students writing seemingly every day. "Just a page," she'd say, "Just a page." That page was a sheet in the ubiquitous spiral-bound notebooks where students wrote down important things their teachers said. Given

Mrs. Winkler's mandate, some students sought wide-ruled notebooks, so a page required fewer words to fill than one in the narrower college-ruled notebooks. Others just wrote with airy letters. Some did both.

For many of my classmates, just a page was a challenge, "Who can write that much?" I could, with ease. For me, Mrs. Winkler's assignments were a challenge of a different sort - to fill no more than just a page, I so full of... words. As Sue once said, "You have a gift for taking a story about nothing and filling a page."

Until this book, my audience has been limited to family and friends, and no longer strangers on social media who've become my unintentional Alpha and Beta readers. Then there are the English teachers, writers, editors, publishers, and Grammar Nazis among those who've contributed, in a more technical way, to make my writing better. To a point, because with readers telling me I write the same way I speak, I don't want to lose my not-always-grammatically correct voice.

While there's a lot not to "Like" about social media, it's given me a platform to write "just a page" more days than not. My "scheduled" posts also provide me with "deadlines" I don't have but need, I often doing my best work when I must. Without them and the resulting stories, I'd be one of those people forever writing but never finishing a book.

This book, the first in a series, contains stories I've been collecting since I can remember, stories I started transcribing in Mrs. Winkler's sixth grade English class, her assignments encouraging me to think about writing one page at a time. A valuable lesson learned because as a journey of a thousand miles starts with a single step, writing a book begins with just a page. So, too, does reading a book, it now your turn...

001

FIRST 14 HOURS

"What the fuck is THAT?"

Gazing out the window of the minibus carrying me and five other new hires on a midnight run across the desert, something monstrous was emerging from the darkness I couldn't identify. Seconds later, I felt foolish when our advancing headlights revealed that THAT was just a roadside billboard, a gigantic cutout of Bibendum, aka The Michelin Tire Man.

Even though I could count the number of hours I'd been in the United Arab Emirates on one hand and still have a few fingers left over, it wasn't the first time since my arrival I'd asked myself the question, as I'd already seen plenty I'd never seen before. I must've had a similar experience the first time I ever opened my eyes, minus the profanity, except this time I had an awareness of who I was, where I was, starting this new life as an adult with 28 years of knowledge and experience to help me find my way. Exhilarating it was.

The day before, though, I wondered what I was doing moving to the Middle East mere months after the Gulf War ended. As my plane climbed into the clouds and the patchwork quilt of Wisconsin countryside disappeared, so did any apprehension. I only had to remind myself why I signed on the dotted line to teach at the national university of the United Arab Emirates - I needed a paycheck.

And I wanted something different, always on the lookout for such after realizing at an early age that if I lived a life like most everyone, I'd get a life like most everyone. So there I sat, continuing my journey on the road less traveled in Seat 3A of a United Express flight from Appleton, Wisconsin, to Chicago's O'Hare Airport.

My 24-hour journey to the UAE was uneventful other than crossing paths with rocker Rod Stewart at a London Heathrow airport magazine stand. As we exchanged greetings, I couldn't help but think Mr. Stewart always had the disheveled look of a man after a long international flight. A look I no doubt shared stepping off the plane in Abu Dhabi and into a stifling combination of midsummer heat and humidity unlike anything I'd ever experienced outside of a sauna, and it was 10 pm.

"Sonofabitch! I was promised no fucking humidity! Son. Of. A. Bitch!" Yes, the first thing I did in the conservative Gulf country was curse, again, and then again, the temperature still over 100 degrees. It was not 100-degree Arizona heat either because Abu Dhabi had humidity. My crotch might not ever dry humidity.

Inside the terminal, air-conditioned, a little old Emirati man awaited holding a "UAE University" sign. He spoke no English, only showing me his list of expected arrivals. After I pointed to my name, he frowned, then grunted, "Curran?" my family name apparently sounding too similar to "Quran." With Gulf Arabs almost always referring to others by their given name, not their family name, they called me "Mister

John," a name I embraced, its formal informality striking a perfect chord.

At the immigration counter, I handed the officer my passport. After thumbing through the pages until he found the relevant one, he gave it an all too thorough examination. Then it was my turn as he aimed his gaze at the back of my head, inquiring with an uncomfortable level of suspicion, "Where did you get this visa?" For the next hour, everyone at immigration asked me the same question, and I gave them all the same answer, "I drew it on the flight over. How's my Arabic?"

OK, that's what I wanted to say. Instead, I said, "I got it from your embassy in Washington, D.C." Where else would I have gotten it? After making my way to the top of the on-duty food chain at immigration that night, I was finally permitted entry into the UAE with a visa I later learned had been made obsolete in the week between when I received it and when I presented it.

After collecting my bags, I was off to customs, where my escort waved off eager inspectors with only the slightest flick of his hand. Outside customs, I met five other hires: an older couple and three single women waiting for me and another couple who had yet to arrive. One of my new colleagues, Anita, a slight young lady with a mountain of luggage, looked at my two smallish checked bags and exclaimed, "Is that all you brought?"

As we waited for the missing couple to show, it began to rain. At least, we thought so until I stepped outside to discover the rain was condensation streaming down the terminal windows - the storm front between the cold, dry air inside and the hot, humid air outside. We watched it "rain" for half an hour until our escort learned the couple we'd been waiting for had turned back at Heathrow. So he herded the six of us onto a minibus for the two-hour ride through the desert to the oasis city of Al Ain, home to our employer and, soon, to all of us.

Along the way, our driver made what I assumed were unscheduled stops at roadside hangouts to join card games. Since gambling was illegal in the UAE, I also assumed the pile of money in the middle of the table must've been a collection for charity. As we waited on the bus, my fellow passengers and I exchanged puzzled looks but nothing more, our voices muted by the uncertainty of our new situation, only hours old.

All we knew was where we were going: to Al Ain's InterContinental Hotel, one of two hotels, the Hilton the other, where the university housed new hires until they settled into their new homes. So after I read the "Welcome to the United Arab Emirates - City of Al Ain" sign, the half written in English, not Arabic, my anticipation grew.

And grew.

And grew because the hotel was on the far side of the sprawling city of 180,000 bordering the Sultanate of Oman. With the drive across Al Ain almost as long as the drive across the desert, my excitement had faded by the time we reached the InterCon. Half-past tired, I just wanted to sleep as it was half-past two and we were to be downstairs for breakfast at six with a busy morning ahead of us.

My "wake-up call" came around five. At first, I thought it was someone in the next room until I remembered there was no next room because I was at the end of the hall. Stumbling around in the dark, trying to locate the source, I discovered someone had left the radio on, the broadcast of the morning call to prayer jump-starting my day and my heart.

As our bleary-eyed group shuffled to the restaurant for breakfast, we appeared to be the hotel's only guests. Not surprising since it was so early and no one stayed in the UAE during the summer if they could avoid it. This was especially true in Al Ain, where daytime temperatures could top 120F and nighttime temps were often in triple digits, but it was the dry heat I was promised.

We made our way to a table for six, but just as I was about to sit down, two waiters whooshed me away, informing me that as a single man, I couldn't sit with a married couple, much less three unmarried women. So, for all our meals that week, I smiled and waved at the others from my private table in the bachelor's section across the otherwise empty restaurant.

At seven, we were back on the minibus. A Sudani woman from the university, Ms. Olfat, who would be our escort for the first week, joined us. Her English was good. We had no trouble understanding her muttering at having to waste her time taking us to the local government hospital for physical exams because "Half of you are going to fail your AIDS test."

Our first stop was for chest X-rays at a clinic next to the hospital. I was surprised but amused to see a lit cigarette dangling from the mouth of our radiologist as she took our chest pictures. With a cough that sounded as though it originated in her bowels, I was dying to ask when she last had a chest X-ray.

After getting our lungs photographed, we made our way to the hospitals, with an "s" as Al Jimi Hospital was really two - one for "mens" and the other for "womens." Unlike the dining room at the InterCon, I would not be alone this time as Gordon, the married man, joined me on the "blue" side while his wife, the three single ladies, and Ms. Olfat were off to the "pink" side. Ms. Olfat sent the Pakistani minibus driver with us, although he had no idea what we were supposed to do and didn't know a word of English. Gordon and I countered by not knowing a word of Urdu.

New to a foreign country, the last place I wanted to be was in a dodgy-looking hospital that reminded me of the grungy basement locker room at the old Waupaca Armory. Looking around, with a tingle traveling the length of my spine, I expected to hear a voice on the intercom say, "Paging Dr. Mengele... Dr. Mengele, please report to the examination room... Dr. Mengele."

A Pakistani bus driver and two whiter-than-white men - a cowboy boot-wearing gent from Wyoming and me - made an unlikely trio until the bus driver wandered off. While he was no help, he was a familiar and friendly face, why we wished he'd stayed. Nevertheless, our stress level subsided once Gordon and I realized that as long as we had a pulse and did not have AIDS, we were going to pass our physicals.

After getting this examined here and that examined there, we discovered that we needed to go to the women's hospital to tick the last box on our list, the eye exam. That we found the exam room was enough for us to pass the eye test, fitting since the eye doctor's assistant appeared nearly blind in the one eye not rolling around in her head.

Thinking our physical examinations were complete, we were relieved until a doctor presented each member of our group, as a group, males and females, with white paper bags. Inside were the items necessary to collect a stool sample. Given the public way he gave us the bags, I wasn't sure if it was homework or his twisted idea of a team-building activity. It was homework.

Our spirits improved during our next stop, at the university's off-campus administrative offices, to pick up our housing allowances meant to help us furnish our villas. The nice, nice lady behind the desk handed me 25,000 Dirhams (almost $7,000), the most money I'd ever held in my hand, even if it was a check. With each of us collecting our stipend, no one cared we lost the use of the minibus for the rest of the day, even though the seven of us would pile into a car meant to seat only four uncomfortably.

I felt fortunate to get the shotgun window seat because the car's air-conditioning didn't work on a typical scorching summer day in Al Ain as we headed downtown to open bank accounts so we could deposit our checks. Rolling through the Clock Tower Roundabout, the heart of downtown, a pickup truck with a camel in the back pulled alongside, the ladies in the backseat squealing when the camel craned its neck, stuck its head through my open window, and kissed me right on the lips.

"Welcome to Al Ain, Mister John!"

Arriving at the Bank of Credit and Commerce Emirates, I got yet another reminder that I wasn't in Wisconsin, as if I needed one, with the Bank Melli Iran located across the street. We arrived to find the front doors of the BCCE locked owing to a combination of bankers' and summer hours. No worries, our escort took us around to the back door. A knock resulted in a man on the other side opening the door, ever so slightly.

"Yes?"

"We're from the university."

Hearing that, the man flung the door open and invited us in. Once the requisite pleasantries had taken place, he offered us tea and biscuits (cookies). Within minutes, we'd all opened accounts and deposited our checks, ending what would be the only pleasant experience I'd ever have at the BCCE.

After the bank, we were off to Etisalat, then the UAE's telecom monopoly, where we completed applications to install telephones in homes we'd not yet seen. Etisalat staff told us to ignore the part on the application where it asked for a street address - Al Ain having no street addresses - residents instead describing most locations relative to the nearest roundabout, each with its own identifying trait.

When one of the single ladies asked how she could tell the fire department where to go if her villa was on fire, I responded, "You could tell them to go to the roundabout nearest your home and look for smoke ... or a frantic woman running up and down the streets screaming FIRE! ...if you knew Arabic." She didn't think that was funny. While Etisalat had already assigned us numbers to telephones that weren't installed in villas we'd not yet seen, after that remark, I knew I'd never get her number. And I didn't.

Our final stop for the morning was UAE University, the Men's Campus, anyway, as government-run colleges and universities had separate campuses for male and female students. The first person I met was in management, a classy Lebanese lady, Paule, who, after giving me the once over, announced her on-the-spot decision that I'd be a distraction to female students by telling me, "You'll never teach on the Women's Campus!" Then she introduced herself. Apparently, I cleaned up better when I was 28.

After I told Brenda about my impending move to the UAE, she told me, "I knew your life was going to be different... not this different." After my first 14 hours in the UAE, it was, so much so that I knew there'd be no turning back. Why I wonder if the couple that turned back at Heathrow ever look back, wondering what they missed.

002

LAST FIRST DATE

Just two blocks from my Sharjah apartment building, the bright red Volkswagen Beetle (version 2.0) caught my eye, and then the driver as she made her way inside after parking next to the office building where Rania worked. Interested, interested, the next time Rania called, I asked if she knew who the babe in the red Beetle was. She did, the young lady a colleague at ALICO (American Life Insurance COmpany).

Rania provided the relevant details - her name was Sawsan, she was Lebanese, not Muslim (my heart broken too many times to go down that road again), and single. Having told Rania months before of the breakup with my Iranian/Emirati, Muslim, and now involved with someone else former girlfriend, she'd been encouraging me to move on. Even though she saw no reason for me not to "move on" her colleague, Rania - Palestinian, Muslim, former student, and single - couldn't play matchmaker because explaining our relationship would've proved problematic.

With Rania having helped all she could, I did something I'd never done - I cold-called Sawsan, in person, "bumping into" her as she left work one evening. Our first encounter was… awkward, probably more so for her, as we chatted between cars in the off-street parking lot. Knowing more than I should've nearly ended that encounter after I asked her name, she replying, "Susan," and I correcting her, asking, "Sawsan?"

Figuring a Westerner wouldn't know the name, her name, she was suspicious until I explained I'd taught Emirati women for years and was familiar with Arab given names. She laughed, then explained she always said her name was Susan when meeting Westerners because it was easier, most not knowing the name Sawsan.

With our encounter still teetering, I didn't hesitate to bring my A-game, presenting her with some of my homemade cookies - that's my A-game. While Sawsan was impressed, at least with my cookies, she sampling some when it was my turn to talk, we never got beyond a couple-two-three chats. Much as I wanted to see where we might go, I had reservations, one of the many voices in my head saying Sawsan wasn't the one, nor was I for her.

Days after deciding Sawsan Road was a likely dead end, I'd have another opportunity, courtesy of Christine, a former colleague at UAE University, who, like me, had taken a job at the Higher Colleges of Technology - she in Abu Dhabi, me in Sharjah. Always the matchmaker, CC wanted to fix me up with one of her colleagues as we gathered at Dubai's Jumeirah Beach Hotel for the HCT's system-wide conference to kick off the 2001-2002 school year.

However, the night before we were to meet, I had dinner at the hotel with CC and another of her Abu Dhabi colleagues, a woman named Leah. There was mutual interest, so plans changed, CC wondering how she missed seeing a Leah/John matchup, one she thought made much more sense than her first fixer-upper.

After the after-dinner conversation, after Leah and I arranged to meet the following week in Abu Dhabi for dinner and a movie, she excused herself to her room while CC and I remained as we had some catching up to do. During our boisterous exchanges, there was a hushed one - when CC confided Leah was about to transfer from a VP position at HCT HQ in Abu Dhabi to the number-two position at, after transferring, my new workplace, Dubai Women's College. If your inquiring mind wants to know, no, Leah wouldn't have been my boss. She would've been my boss' boss' boss.

While that would've been… interesting, maybe too interesting, HCT should've put Leah in charge of Dubai Women's College, the system a good ole boys club when it came to directors. With the HCT divided into men's and women's campuses and the overwhelming majority of the system's enrollment women, a female director at a women's college would've made sense, probably why there'd never been one.

As arranged, Leah and I saw Shrek at the Marina Mall cinema the next week with dinner in the food court afterward. On our first date, nothing went wrong, but nothing went either. Neither did her relationship with DWC, the deal falling through, and I never saw her again as she moved back to the States. I like to think we were the right people, just not for each other. Last I checked, Dr. Leah was a community college president married to a shutterbug like me.

They say the third time's the charm, and it would come the next week as I had my third first date that month with a neighbor, a former colleague at Sharjah Women's College. We'd gotten to know each other while hitching rides to work and back with a Bahraini colleague who lived in our apartment building. We got to know each other even better after learning we shared an interest in buying a Jeep, Wranglers we would buy together, along with her long-time friends from Canada, Sally and Don, at the dealer in Dubai off Airport Road.

Months before, on January 28, 2001, the day after I moved to the UAE for the second time, she and I met in an elevator lobby. Having arrived in the UAE two weeks before me, she'd already moved in as I and some other new hires were getting a tour of what would soon be our new home, the Canal Building, an apartment block on Sharjah's Qasbah Canal. Yes, we met at the Qasbah. That's where I... caught her eye.

While we remember that first encounter, at the time, she still had a boyfriend in Calgary, Alberta, and I'd not yet discovered that after 18 months apart, my girlfriend had moved on, so neither she nor I were paying much attention. At least I wasn't, but one heartbreak, one lost job, and seven months later, I was, enough my neighbor and I made a date to see a movie at Sharjah's Al Massa Cinema. The movie? *Shrek*. For obvious reasons, I didn't tell her I'd seen it the week before, on another first date. That and I was happy to see *Shrek* a second time... with a neighbor named Sue. To this day, *Shrek* remains the only movie I've ever seen in a theatre, twice.

A Canadian and an American, Sue and I were the only Westerners in attendance. Why, at times, we were the only ones laughing, drawing looks from Easterners who'd missed one of the movie's many American cultural references. Sure, *Shrek* played well across cultures - a green ogre and a talking donkey can do that - but to appreciate some of the movie's more subtle laughers, moviegoers almost had to have grown up in the United States or Canada.

Canadians and Americans are not "same same," as my wife reminds me, and I'm sure I remind her. Nevertheless, with the majority of Canadians hugging the American border in a desperate attempt to stay warm-er, they're exposed, for better or worse, to all the American culture they could ever want. Too bad too many Americans don't take an interest in what Canada offers unless it first moves to the States.

While awkward, one of those times Sue and I laughed alone in the darkened theatre proved illuminating as I thought of past girlfriends from African and Asian countries and wondered, "If so-and-so was sitting beside me, would I be laughing alone, truly alone?" Don't get me wrong, cross-cultural relationships can and do work, and of course, there are plenty of relationships between people who grew up in the same neighborhood that have ended in divorce... or a homicide investigation.

Even so, experience has taught me that when a couple starts in more or less the same place, they have a head start. On our first date, *Shrek* - the movie, not the ogre - underscored Sue and I did indeed have a head start. If nothing else, we had more to discuss afterward over pizza at a restaurant on the ground floor of Rania's office building. But unlike my previous first dates that month, my first date with Sue, my last first date, went... why we're still on it.

003

527 CENTRE STREET

Married, mothered, and divorced before she was old enough to vote, Ma had dug herself a deep hole. Perhaps the best thing she did for me as a child, before getting involved with Del, was find a great babysitter. She didn't have to look far because just a half block over, two blocks down, and another half block over from our apartment was the home of Bob and Susie Stelter, the heart and soul of our neighborhood on Eau Claire's north side.

Theirs was a two-story house with an open porch out front and a screened one out back. On the first floor was a kitchen big enough for a table and eight chairs, a dining room big enough for a never-used table and eight chairs, a living room, a powder room, and a foyer.

"Ma, how come we don't have a foyer?

"We don't need one."

"Ma, what's a foyer?"

Upstairs, there were four bedrooms. Bob and Susie's was on the left at the top of the stairs. I don't think I ever set foot in that room, even though nobody told me not to. Across the hall was Amy's bedroom, which featured a canopy bed, a stuffed animal zoo, and pink. At the end of the hall on the left was the bedroom of their oldest child, Robbie, and across the hall was the bedroom of their youngest, Tommy. Sandwiched between was a bathroom that featured, after a late '60s renovation, avocado green.

The basement was the one place in the house where the brick chimney for the furnace was visible, where I decided there was no Santa Claus because there was no way an old fat guy was getting down that. And even if he did, where would he go? Into the furnace? Because he sure couldn't squeeze through that little metal door at the bottom of the bricks.

The washer and dryer were down there, along with a large concrete double laundry sink used to wash cucumbers when Susie canned pickles each summer. There was also a toilet and a shower down there, but I don't think anyone ever used them, maybe because neither stall had a door to keep out the spiders.

While the front yard was typical city-lot small, the backyard was good-sized. In the northeast corner, decreasingly covered in peeling bluish-gray paint, was an old wooden barn called "the garage." Even though I never saw a vehicle parked inside, it made for a great Halloween spookhouse.

Rummaging through the clutter in the garage every summer, a bunch of us kids managed to find the necessary parts to almost build a go-cart. While we had plenty of rusty, hammered-straight nails, we always seemed to come up a wheel or board short of competing with General Motors. But we still had our bicycles - mine, a 20-inch Schwinn, metallic blue, with a banana seat, butterfly handlebars, and racing slick back tire. When the gang was riding, we were our own parade.

The backdrop to Bob and Susie's backyard was Longfellow Elementary, my kindergarten, first, and second-grade school. Located mid-block, just like Bob and Susie's house, the red brick three-story building and adjoining asphalt-covered playgrounds occupied the other half of the block, except for a few homes on the north side. The only buffer between Bob and Susie's lot and the school grounds was the alley bisecting the block into east and west halves.

Bob worked downtown at the Uniroyal Tire factory. A burly man with a five o'clock shadow at every hour of the day, Bob seldom wore anything other than blue jeans and a T-shirt with a single left-side pocket, almost always a pack of smokes tucked under his left sleeve. His tightly cropped dark hair and dark glasses with a heavy plastic frame suited him perfectly.

After working a late shift at Uniroyal, Bob often came home to a house full of mostly not his kids, yet I never saw him lose his temper. He was a patient, patient man, but those few times he maybe wouldn't have been, he had a subtle way of letting everyone know to steer clear. And all the kids did. Respect. And there could be a slew of kids because Susie ran a daycare center out of her home. While there was no actual business, no sign out front, and no advertising other than word of mouth, there were many mouths as Susie looked after as many as 30 children.

And their two dogs, Pugsley and Mitzi. Pugsly was a gray poodle and, like Bob, patient with the kids, just a good dog. Mitzi was a rust-colored Chihuahua who spent most of her day hiding under the sofa, growling at anyone who dared make eye contact with her fiery reds. While Mitzi often looked like she wanted to bite anyone and everyone, as far as I know, she never did. Instead, it was one of Susie's charges that once bit Mitzi.

All three of their children were older than I was, although Tommy was only seven months older. He and

I grew up together as Susie started taking care of me when I was two years old because, in addition to going to school full-time at the University of Wisconsin-Eau Claire, Ma also worked full-time. As a result, she didn't have much time to raise me, but she couldn't have found two better people to look after her only child than Bob and Susie.

While they had help from my grandparents and some of my aunts and uncles, Susie, a bubbly extrovert, was quite the contrast to Bob, but the two made a perfect pair, contributing to my early childhood development as much as anyone. They were my adopted parents... adopted by me. Until Ma and I moved to Waupaca just before my ninth birthday, Bob and Susie's home was my home away from home because I probably spent more awake time there than in my own.

With Bob having a good blue-collar job at the factory and Susie babysitting so many kids, they could afford the niceties Ma could not. Their RCA console color TV was the first I'd ever seen. While we got just the one channel on our 13-inch black-and-white Motorola, their TV got many as they had a steel tower topped by an aerial on a rotor to watch channels from far off and mysterious places called Minneapolis and LaCrosse. But we didn't sit and watch TV all day, as there was too much to do. Besides, even their TV didn't get that many channels.

With Susie looking after so many children, we ate in shifts, little ones first so they could get to their naps. The older ones helped Susie make and serve lunch. The only one in the house the kids didn't help make meals for was Bob, as Susie took care of that. Quite often, it was fried hamburgers with onions. While it would've been breakfast for me, it was dinner for Bob after he worked the night shift at Uniroyal. I'll never forget the aroma that filled the kitchen as Bob's burgers sizzled on the stove.

"Ma, why don't we have burgers and onions for breakfast?"

Susie also tasked us with cleaning up the house and after ourselves, which was a never-ending chore. In the fall, we raked leaves. In the winter, we shoveled snow from the walks and the driveway. We even did some of the grocery shopping. With a book of trading stamps, a few bucks, and a list, Susie'd send us on mission quests to Holiday, a gas station/convenience store a few blocks away.

And back then, with gas priced at nineteen-nine a gallon, a couple of bucks went a long way when Susie pulled up to the pump in their early '60s model Cadillac, navy blue, with tail fins… and a couple dozen kids stuffed inside like an oversized clown car. I always wondered what the attendant thought when Susie shouted above the din, "Two dollars of regular, please."

And it was always "please" and "thank you" because manners were required. There'd be trouble if the Golden Rule was ever broken at Bob and Susie's home. Since no one wanted to find out what that trouble would be, on those rare occasions when there was a problem, we worked it out amongst ourselves, away from the adults.

On special days, like someone's birthday, we'd get to buy a case of soda pop, or pop, or soda at Holiday. Susie always instructed us to buy the store brand variety case of 24 cans so, hopefully, every kid could drink the flavor they preferred… which never happened. The cans were white with different colored polka dots matching the artificial color and flavor of the drink inside - purple for grape, brown for root beer, red for cherry, yellow for cream soda, green for lemon-lime, and orange for... well, you get the idea. They were colors even the kid who got held back a year could name, colors found in the 8-box of Crayola Crayons.

Of the 24 mixed-flavor cans, the lemon limes (the equivalent of 7-Up or Sprite) were always the last cans we chose, but they were still more popular than either can of cola (the equivalent of Coke or Pepsi) that no one ever chose. They'd stand alone in the cardboard flat until Friday night when some adult added them to something called rum. I don't know what color the polka dots were on the cola cans, but it wasn't a color found in the 8-box of Crayolas. I'm not sure it would've been found in a 64-box either.

So what happens to children that when they become adults, they choose Coke and Pepsi, the flavor they wouldn't drink as children, along with 7Up and Sprite, the flavor they would grudgingly choose only because there was nothing else except for the cola? To this day, I still drink what I mostly drank as a kid - water, straight from the tap... or a garden hose.

If we had a few coins in our pockets, sometimes we'd walk to Timber's Grocery, across the street from Holiday. A mom-and-pop operation at the intersection of Birch and McDonough Streets, Jack Timber and his wife owned and operated the corner store and lived in the small apartment upstairs. We went to Timber's because they had a much better selection of candy than Holiday, but with so many choices, plus all the negotiating over what candy we would share and what we would not, sometimes it took us half an hour to figure out how to spend 25 cents. Like Bob, Jack was a patient, patient man.

While Bob and Susie worked hard, they played hard, too, usually on Friday nights. They, along with

Ma and other assorted family and friends, partied at places like Wagner's 40½ Bowling Lanes, The Chicken Chaser's, or The Diamond Lounge, owned by Susie's brother-in-law, the catcher on a local fast-pitch softball team, one of the best in the country. On those Friday nights, whatever kids would have no adult supervision stayed at Bob and Susie's. Late into the night, we'd watch scary movies from the safety of our blanket forts... OK, Bob and Susie's dining room table and chairs occasionally got used.

To get us out of the house Saturday morning, the adults handed each of us a buck or two to pay for a day at one of the movie theaters in downtown Eau Claire. While the parents enjoyed some quiet time and Alka-Seltzer at home, we'd watch cartoons, The Three Stooges, and then a G-rated movie, maybe two, before walking back with stomachs full of popcorn and Milk Duds. Given the number of kids in the theatre, many parents in Eau Claire played hard on Friday nights.

In the summer, Bob and Susie liked to go up north, staying at resorts alongside Wisconsin's many lakes, they often inviting me. Those trips were even more fun after Bob and Susie bought a bus. A bus! It was an old motor coach, one of those rounded airstream types. It needed a lot of work to convert it from passenger service to a recreational vehicle. While Bob and his buddies did the interior renovation, outfitting it with all the comforts of a typical recreational vehicle - kitchen, bathroom, dining area, and beds - we were tasked with scraping the old paint and rust, mostly rust, from the sides of the bus.

We did a good job for a bunch of kids, as the bus looked brand new after a two-tone paint job - forest green in a band around the windows, while the rest matched Bob and Susie's avocado-colored upstairs bathroom. Given the paint job, we affectionately referred to the bus as "The Jolly Green Giant." With two big round headlights on either side of its grill, it had a jolly face.

Decades later, I spotted the bus parked in a field off Highway 12 just east of the small town of Altoona, just east of Eau Claire. With a "FOR SALE" sign in its front window, I was happy to know The Jolly Green Giant was still around. The joy of seeing an old friend faded though as the years passed and the bus went unsold, its green paint rusting, and I knowing the effort made by a backyard army of kids to restore the bus to its green grandeur of the late '60s would not be repeated.

Even so, seeing the bus brought back all the good memories of Bob and Susie. After so many years, one that stood out more than most was me standing in their backyard watching the jets pass overhead on their way to or from the Minneapolis airport, 80 miles away as the jet flies. Looking up, I wondered what the world looked like from so high in the sky. And what could be so far away people needed to fly? "Someday, I'll find out."

The buildings Timber's Grocery and Holiday once occupied are still standing. I laughed the last time I drove by as Timber's was John's Computer Repair while Holiday was Sue's Bakery. Driving by Bob and Susie's, though, tears filled my eyes as only the memories remained, the house, garage, and yard... all gone, replaced with, appropriately enough, I suppose, a playground. To make way for an addition to Longfellow Elementary, as well as more playgrounds, playing fields, and a parking lot, all the houses on the block were demolished, including what was Bob and Susie's home at 527 Centre Street.

21

004

THOSE WITH ILLINOIS PLATES

"YOU ~~CENSORED~~!"

Horns were honking. Fists were shaking. Fingers were flying. Enjoying the show in his driver's side mirror, my Uncle David was grinning from ear to ear, while my Uncle Mike, assessing the situation from the passenger side, had more of a diabolical smirk, like the Grinch as he hatched his plot to stop Christmas from coming to Whoville. Me? Sitting between my uncles, with views to both side mirrors, I laughed so hard my guts hurt.

That sunny summer day, the three of us shared the bench seat in a box truck from the A-1 Rental Center. After living most of my nearly nine years at 417½ McDonough Street on Eau Claire's north side, it was moving day, our destination, Box 19F, Lawson Drive, on Waupaca's east side, a dead-end road development of 15 cookie-cutter houses. The move was necessary as Ma was soon to start her first teaching job, at Waupaca High School.

Ma, her sister and David's wife, Rita, were ahead of us in Ma's car, a sky-blue Plymouth Fury III. Way ahead because Ma, like her father, had a lead foot, while the A-1 Rental truck had a governor. If you don't know what a governor is, this kind, anyway, it's a device that restricts how fast a vehicle can go. Apparently, the people at A-1 were familiar with the expression "driven like a rented mule" because the truck's top speed was limited to 45mph. With a 65mph speed limit on most Wisconsin highways, Ma and Rita would complete the 150-mile journey long before we would.

Putting aside thoughts about the friends and family in the Eau Claire area I'd be leaving behind or what awaited me in a new neighborhood and school in Waupaca, moving day was exciting. So was riding in a truck, something I'd never done before, an experience the governor extended. As did the highways between Eau Claire and Waupaca because almost all were the two-lane variety, so the going was going to be slow anyway.

After making the ten-mile trip north on Highway 53 to Chippewa Falls, the divided highway ended a short way out of town, heading east on Highway 29. Except for short bits of divided highway on either side of Wausau and just north of Stevens Point, two lanes were all there were. Highway 29 was a miserable road, narrow but straight, so drivers could see the oncoming traffic that eliminated any hope of passing. Bad as it was in summer, it was worse in winter, the east/west road unprotected from blowing snow with farm fields on either side.

The drive from Wausau to Stevens Point on Highway 51 was usually better in winter, the road mostly flanked by forest, but in summer, it was bad. A major north/south artery in a state attracting throngs of tourists from Illinois, Highway 51, like Highway 53 north of Eau Claire, was almost always bumper-to-bumper with FIBs (Fucking Illinois Bastards) in RVs and campers, often towing trailers with boats and whatever else they needed to enjoy their homes away from home.

(NOTE: Having read an early draft of this story, Marte, one of the first friends I made after moving to Waupaca, and a longtime resident of Wisconsin's north woods, told me of another applicable acronym I'd not heard before - FISHTAB (Fucking Illinois Shit Head Towing A Boat). Even though Wisconsinites only refer to their southern neighbors as FIBs, or even FISHTABs, with the greatest affection, I thought FISHTAB... harsh, so I left it out of this story.)

Such recreational obstacles were almost impossible to pass. They were wide and/or long, and there was always oncoming traffic. Even if a driver could get around, the line ahead was so long it wouldn't make much difference, why it took longer than it should've to go almost anywhere in summer. Even more aggravating, all those tourists had such happy faces, what with their singing songs and playing games like Slug Bug and I Spy as they cheerily chugged along, oblivious to all those stuck behind them.

"If you moved here, you'd already be here!"

Clogging the highways as if they had every right to, as if they paid taxes, they never pulled over. They never turned onto another highway, needed gas, food, or a restroom, and never just crashed into a ditch or one of the countless trees lining the highway. Never. So, even with only a few years of backseat driving experience, I'd already spent far too much of my life staring at boat propellers through car windshields. If only there was a way to exact revenge on those tourists from Illinois. If only there was a way...

Heading south on Highway 51, not far out of Wausau, my uncles and I noticed the line of vehicles behind our A-1 Rental truck was growing...

"Wow! Look at all those RV's, campers, and boats!"

And growing impatient. Every now and then, someone would pull out to pass, but the oncoming traffic put them back in their place, behind us. There was just no getting around our boxy A-1 Rental truck. Eventually, the line got so long we couldn't see the tail end in the side-view mirrors.

Even though David was doing his best to eke out 45mph from the governor-restricted truck, it was still 20mph below the posted speed limit, one many Illinois drivers viewed as merely a recommendation and one on the low side at that. Why Mike thought it might be fun to…

"Drop it down to 40. See what happens."

What happened was we felt better about not being able to go faster by going slower, those behind us now at the mercy of David's right foot as it eased off the accelerator. Revenge! Revenge for all the times we'd been stuck behind them and couldn't do a thing about it. Now we were laughing, howling, mocking the highly agitated reflections in the side-view mirrors, they honking their horns, shaking their fists, and flying their fingers as they shouted for us to…

"Drop it down to 30. See what happens."

Mike would marry Alice a year later, her positive influence perhaps saving the world from destruction had Mike's diabolical plots continued to go unchecked.

All good things must end, as did our revenge tour when the divided portion of the highway began just north of Stevens Point. Those who'd been stuck behind us for 20 or so miles couldn't get around us fast enough. If Smokey had been there with a radar gun, he could've pulled over everyone, even those that slowed as they passed to shout still more "words of encouragement."

Some were thoughtful enough to use hand gestures in case we couldn't hear. Those with Illinois plates were particularly courteous.

As the tail end of the vehicles that had been stuck behind us passed, we turned off Highway 51 onto Highway 10 and headed east toward Waupaca, 25 miles away. Just a dozen miles from what would be my new home, but almost out of gas, David pulled into a roadside red-brick Texaco station in the unincorporated town of Custer. As the man who wore the star filled the truck's tank, we delighted in our first opportunity to relive every epic mile of revenge we exacted between Wausau and Stevens Point.

We finally arrived in Waupaca that afternoon, well after Ma and Rita, but with a memory we always recalled fondly. These days, it's just a memory, as our route is now freeway, all the way, including Highway 51. But every time I'm on that stretch between Wausau and Stevens Point, I remember moving day, August 9, 1971, when there was one governor, two lanes, the three of us, and countless RVs, campers, and boats trailing behind.

005

BOY!

Growing up in small-town Wisconsin, I never knew what it was to be a minority, but as a member of the University of Florida football team, that's exactly what I was because of the 140 or so players on the team, I was the only one... from Wisconsin. With nearly all of my teammates from either Florida or Georgia, they seemed fascinated someone from the Badger State had joined the Gators. So they asked questions, some that made me think they thought Wisconsin, instead of another state, another country.

While there were the requisite jerks on and around the football team, overall, most were welcoming and friendly toward the "foreign exchange student" from Wisconsin. Outside of my position group (kickers), my best friends on the team were fellow freshmen, offensive tackle Lomas Brown and linebacker Alonzo Johnson. Good guys and players, both would be named All-Americans at their respective positions and go on to have professional football careers.

Alonzo and I got to know each other in the athletic dorm before practice, over a pool table, we often the only two in an otherwise empty lounge. Alonzo liked to play pool and was good at it. I liked to play pool.

"Wolfie, you suck!"

The other players called me Wolfie because I had long hair, which also made me a minority on the team, as I was the only one who did. Given the heat and humidity of Florida, my teammates sported buzz cuts, or at least short hair, never really getting their heads wrapped around my mop-top, although one asked, "Is that how people up north stay warm?"

Playing pool against Alonzo helped me become a better player, and so did Alonzo, he tutoring me on the finer points of the game so I could at least make him work for a win. I got better, never good enough to beat him, but good enough to give Alonzo a good game occasionally, so at least he saw some return on his investment.

Lomas and I got to know each other on the practice field, even though he was an offensive tackle, kickers often "volunteered" to man the first down markers for the offense after we were done kicking for the day. Working on the chain gang proved fun while providing us a front-row seat to watch the offense practice.

The show's star was not a player but the offensive coordinator, a young hotshot named Mike Shanahan. No one knew then he would go on to win two Super Bowls as head coach of the Denver Broncos, but as driven as any man I've ever met, it didn't surprise me when he did. His first Super Bowl win, over the heavily favored Green Bay Packers, was tough for me to take. The sting of the unexpected loss was somewhat lessened because a former coach of mine had now won a Super Bowl, and then two, when Denver won again the following year.

Coach Shanahan was a Type-A personality if ever there was one, A+ even. He rubbed some people the wrong way because he expected everyone else to be a Type-A, too, A+ even. While his intensity seemed a square peg in the round hole that was the laid-back culture at Florida, it did make for some entertaining football practices.

Despite his slight stature, Mike could scream almost as loudly as I could, and I could decalcify your body. Whenever one of his offensive charges failed to execute a play according to his high standard (perfection), he'd scream, "ON THE LINE! RUN IT AGAIN!" as his head would rattle and steam like a pressure cooker. With a young team, he screamed, "ON THE LINE! RUN IT AGAIN!" seemingly every play. After spotting a player who'd botched his assignment, sometimes the chain gang beat Coach Shanahan to the punch, "ON THE LINE! RUN IT AGAIN!" we silently mouthing the words just before Mike exploded out loud.

Even as a true freshman, Lomas was the team's starting right tackle. At six-foot-four and nearly 300 pounds, he probably would've led my high school football team to a state championship - "Run behind Lomas!" For many years, former Detroit Lions and Hall of Fame running back Barry Sanders did - that he retired as the NFL's second all-time leading rusher spoke to the talent of both men. But on the practice field at the University of Florida, Lomas was a frequent target of Coach Shanahan's maniacal, bug-eyed rants.

While Lomas had size and talent, as a freshman, he also had a lot to learn, and Coach Shanahan never let him forget that. During breaks, Lomas provided us with commentary between several well-deserved swigs of Gatorade - a sports drink developed at Florida - once muttering, "One day I'm gonna CENSORED!" Coach Shanahan just wanted Lomas to be the best he could be, something I'm sure Lomas appreciates now after a stellar 18-year NFL career.

In my friendships with Alonzo and Lomas, I was the white guy. I didn't mention it before because it didn't matter. On the team, what did was performance, as evidenced by Coach Shanahan's rants. I mention color now because once we stepped outside the locker room, some judged my teammates and me on what didn't and shouldn't matter.

Like Willy, a good old boy I worked with at Beerworld, a self-serve gas station, minimart, car wash, and, oh, yes, a place that sold not only a lot of beer but more beer brands than any other store in Gainesville. Just a couple blocks down the hill from campus, many of Beerworld's customers were UF students, including some who shouldn't have been. Like the co-ed scanning the beer coolers one Friday night who proclaimed to her equally ditzy friend, "Oh look! Moosehead Beer! Just like the T-shirts!"

I was delighted to see others enter the store, like Roger Maris, the local Budweiser distributor and former New York Yankees baseball player. In 1961, Roger broke Babe Ruth's single-season home run record with 61 round-trippers, a record Maris held until the 2022 season, in my book anyway. Yet, for all the steroid-infused players who "broke" Ruth's record after Roger, only he got an asterisk - his homers hit in a 162-game season, Ruth's in a 154.

Then there were those I hoped would never enter the store, as armed robberies were common in Gainesville. Like trailer parks for tornados, convenience stores were popular targets. Every Saturday night, my co-workers and I had an informal pool on when, not if, someone would rob the Majik Market on the corner across the street.

That pool ended after a robber shot a clerk there. Why, when Willy worked the register at Beerworld, he kept a Dirty Harry-sized handgun under the counter, one of those blow-your-head-clean-off type weapons. When I inquired, he had no shame in telling me, "Yeah, I hope one of them "n-words" tries to rob us cuz I wanna shoot me one… dead," it not a robber he wanted to kill.

Willy's racism was the most blatant and unapologetic I experienced living in Florida as the prejudice just spewed from his hate hole. I preferred such obvious racists, though, because they were easier to identify and avoid over those who expressed their prejudice in more subtle, often hypocritical ways.

While Willy was happy to share his opinions, the more refined practitioners of hate were harder to spot, but I soon discovered I could while standing in line waiting for service. When the person behind the counter looked like me, I was treated with stereotypical Southern hospitality, "How y'all doing today?" But where was that charming personality just minutes earlier when the person at the head of the line didn't look like me and was treated rather rudely? That was no way to treat a customer. That was no way to treat anyone.

I found this insidious form of racism far more frustrating than Willy's cartoonish variety, and I was just a witness, so I can only imagine how a lifetime on the receiving end of such soul-crushing treatment must feel. Never working the register, I never had the chance to treat everyone the same from behind the counter at Beerworld. I was a stock boy and janitor - the first of eleven consecutive years I would clean toilets for money.

"Toilet whore!" (Sue chiming in…)

Once a month, though, I got outside for the day, responsible for washing the asphalt lot. To help get the job done, in a large, plastic-lined cardboard drum, we had some orange powder that looked like TANG instant orange drink. Maybe it was TANG, which had the same directions - Add water. I'd scatter some powder on an asphalt patch and wet it. After scrubbing the area with a stiff push broom, I'd hose it off, the oil and gas stains disappearing down the storm drain.

One morning, as I was getting started on the high corner of the lot, a car pulled up to the pumps. I'd seen the driver stop before, and I like to think he did so because with stepbrother Jay and/or his wife Jean working the register during the day, I know he was treated like everyone else. While filling his tank, a university student on a bicycle cut the corner on his way up the hill toward campus. For no other reason than to demonstrate his ignorance, as he pedaled past the man at the pump, the bicyclist made a derisive remark.

"BOY!"

Still holding the nozzle, the man at the pump looked up. Even from across the lot, I could see his disgust as this punk pedaled on, laughing, believing that on his bike, he could get away and get away with his "crime." But as the bicyclist approached, somehow... the hose... got away from me... spraying that overly satisfied smirk right off his face. So startled by the unexpected hosing, he lost control of his bike, crashing to the asphalt as the contents of his backpack scattered. By the time I... regained control of the hose... he was soaked, as were his books and papers.

"WHAT THE FUCK ARE YOU DOING?"

"Just cleaning the slime on our lot. Now I suggest you get on outta here before that "boy" comes over here and kicks your ass, and I help."

Realizing how vulnerable he was, with his bike no longer under his boney butt and the target of his cowardly remark only a sprint away, he thought better of making more trouble, hurriedly gathering himself and his soggy belongings before hightailing it up the street. Having shown himself to be a coward, I had no worries he'd return to exact revenge, nor that I'd face any repercussions over my actions. Now, if I'd been black…

Instead, I was a privileged character, even more so as a member of the University of Florida football team. Not only did my team polo shirt get me immediate seating at The Brown Derby restaurant on 32-ounce Porterhouse Night, but if the cyclist had called the cops, the only punishment I might've faced would've come not from the judicial system but from coaches, making me run stadium steps after practice for forcing them to clean up my mess.

Privilege, yes, but I like to think when faced with another abusing theirs, I took proper advantage of mine. Privilege so ingrained that I acted as I did without considering the consequences, without having to consider them. Not that I had much time to, the situation at Beerworld unfolding in seconds, but I didn't need those seconds because I was who I was. Now, if I'd been black…

Once the racist on two wheels pedaled out of sight, I returned to washing the lot. Glancing over, I saw the man at the pump giving his gas cap a twist before slapping the cover closed. He flashed me a smile, more a grin, along with a nod of approval. What I gave him, if anything, I'll never know, hopefully, a good story to tell his boy.

006

NICE HAT

In the first weeks of my freshman year at the University of Florida, temperatures were often in the 90s, with humidity that could knock a buzzard off a manure wagon. Inside the auditorium, the "weather" could be even worse, why I sat in the back row, near the always-open double doors, to catch whatever breeze there might be. How fitting weather determined the "atmosphere" for the Meteorology 101 class, held in one of the oldest buildings on campus, one without air-conditioning, that worked. Why, with 500 students stuffed inside, I sometimes forgot what I was there to study.

Good thing the casually dressed professor down front reminded me. Good thing he was down front, or I might not have been able to tell him apart from the students, as he wore Hawaiian shirts, cut-offs, and sandals to beat the heat. On the first day of class, he'd made his first impression, wearing a suit and tie befitting his status in academia, but after that, he said he figured his students knew he was the professor, so why not dress for comfort?

Despite his casual attire, he still might've been the best-dressed person in the hot and steamy auditorium, as students also dressed for comfort, I not wearing more than a t-shirt and shorts. Others wore even less, like the young ladies who attended class barely wearing bikinis, giving a whole new meaning to "grading on a curve."

"Johnny, you're not in Waupaca anymore."

In my second year of university, let's just say the "scenery" changed, but not for the better. Sophomore slump? No. The Gators' team doctor recommended I give up football. He didn't like my hips - yadda, yadda, yadda, if you want to walk when you're 40, yadda, yadda yadda. As a result, my life changed course as I changed universities, the next two years, I matriculating at the University of Wisconsin-Platteville, located in the southwest corner of the state. Platteville wasn't the end of the world, but if I'd climbed to the top of the campus bell tower, I could've seen the end, just down the road.

There were no professors in Hawaiian shirts, cut-offs, and sandals on campus. Nor were there girls in bikinis. Or girls. A mining and engineering school, coeds were few at UWP. Why there were jokes: Platteville - where the men are men, the women are men, and the sheep are nervous. What do you call a coed at UWP? Lost. It's why UWP students sometimes road-tripped to Dubuque, Iowa, looking for fun.

Ever wonder what a world largely devoid of women would look like? My time at Platteville was a window to such a world, as I saw grunting, hairy, slovenly, knuckle-dragging third-from-the-right on the evolutionary chart humanoids wandering around between the dorms, cafeteria, lecture halls, and cemetery... but the men were way worse.

"Johnny, you're not in Gainesville anymore."

Perhaps the most visible sign of the lack of women, besides the lack of women, was the "dress code." With few females around to impress, male students dressed for comfort, sweatpants the featured component of the "school uniform." Add whatever shirt was near the top of the clothes pile on the dorm room floor, and students were good to go - to class, the cafeteria, a meeting with the dean, a funeral, a job interview, whatever.

No UWP school uniform was complete without a hat, whether miner, hard, baseball, or stocking. In winter, a headcover was a near necessity, as any walk on the wind-swept campus made freezing to death a real possibility. Nevertheless, I think hats were popular at Platteville because they hid a lot of uncombed, unbrushed, and often unwashed hair. When it wasn't too cold, my chapeau of choice was a blue and orange University of Florida Fighting Gators baseball cap that, coincidentally, matched UW-Platteville's school colors.

After transferring to the University of Wisconsin-Milwaukee, my third university in four years, that tattered, possibly filthy, but ever-present hat topped my ever-present head as I entered Engelmann Hall, home of the School of Architecture and Urban Planning. My first class was Architectural Fundamentals 200, the classroom in the basement of what was a converted elementary school.

As usual, when it was my choice, I sat in the back row to observe the proceedings. The 8 am class began with a roll call at precisely 8 am. As the professor made his way through the alphabetical list of 30 or so names, it didn't take long to get to mine.

"John Curran?"

"Yo!"

Hearing my ill-advised reply, the professor looked up from his ledger. While I was sitting in the back row, the third of three rows of cheap white laminated tables fronting hard plastic chairs, either beige or dirty, I sat in his direct line of sight. With a stone-faced look I hadn't seen since my last visit to Mount Rushmore, he flatlined his reply to my "Yo" with a mocking, "Nice hat," the professor then resuming roll call, without so much as an apology.

"Johnny, you're not in Platteville anymore."

As the saying goes, you never get a second chance to make a first impression. Mine was made with my first word - Yo, and the professor's with his pair - Nice hat. Think back. Can you remember the first words you said to various people in or out of your life? Can you remember their first words to you?

For any you do recall, I'm guessing they were words exchanged with someone who eventually mattered more than most. Given our less-than-stellar start - that the last time I ever wore a hat to his or any other class at UWM - you might think I would've long since forgotten our first exchange, but I still remember. I still remember because Professor Kent Keegan would soon become someone who mattered more than most.

007

DUBAI TO HAIDA GWAII

For the benefit of those (not you, of course) who don't know their Canadian geography as well as long-time *Jeopardy* host (and even longer-time Canuck) Alex Trebek thought they should, Haida Gwaii is located on the west coast of British Columbia just south of the southern end of the Alaskan panhandle. The Haida Nation is the oldest civilization on the North American continent, their history dating back at least 13,000 years, so if you think the world is just 6,000 years old…

Never heard of Haida Gwaii? The "Islands of the People" in the language of the Haida? Formerly known as the Queen Charlotte Islands? One of the last remaining virgin forest archipelagos in the world? Sometimes referred to as "The Galapagos of the North" given its unique biodiversity, similar to the islands off Ecuador's coast? Once the most highly populated area in North America?

No worries, some Canadians have never heard of the place either. Haida Gwaii's under-the-radar status is one reason Sue and I love to visit. Another is that we often wish we were there when we're not. So much so we purchased a home there in 2017 with the idea it would be our next stop after Ecuador.

Another reason is that Haida Gwaii is one of the best fishing holes in the world - in season, with a license, of course. And if we ever get bored catching halibut and trophy salmon, we could always grab a net and go crabbing in the surf off North Beach, or grab a shovel and go digging for razor clams on the beach, in season, with a license, of course. Even if seafood weren't our thing, all we need to go deer hunting on the islands is an apple and a hammer - in season, with a license, of course. Probably don't even need the apple.

With all those fish, lucky for us, Scott and Joanne had a boat. If you've never heard of Scott and Jo, no worries about that either - he's my brother-in-law, and she's his long-time girlfriend. For many years, they had a getaway house on Haida Gwaii, in the town of Masset, parked right next to their boat. Even though the town has only 800 or so residents, with fewer than 5000 people living on the 154-island archipelago (only two are permanently populated), that's almost enough to make Masset the largest metro area on the islands.

Perhaps because there aren't so many residents to spread the word about what a great place Haida Gwaii is, overrun it's not. Not, even though the rainforest scenery, mountains, rivers, lakes, inlets, islands, coves, beaches, bays, abundant wildlife, and Haida culture scream of a place that should be crawling with residents and tourists alike. Until July 2006, Sue and I had only heard of Haida Gwaii, which was about to become one of our favorite places.

First, we had to get there because we were living and working in the United Arab Emirates, so we had a long way to go - 10,000 miles as the crow flies. However, we'd be flying KLM and Northwest. Due to the heat, international flights to Europe typically departed the UAE in the middle of the night, so we spent most of the day racing the sun as we traveled west, our journey beginning with a nine-hour flight from Dubai to Amsterdam. After a layover, there was another nine-hour flight to Minneapolis, then another layover, followed by a three-hour flight to Calgary, where the sun finally passed us upon our arrival.

Sue's father, Art, met us at the airport and then drove us to his home in the Haysboro neighborhood at the city's opposite end. After consuming only airplane and airport food over the previous 30 hours, we welcomed a proper home-cooked meal. After dinner was done, Sue and I retreated to the bedroom… wait for it… to repack our bags for the trip to Haida Gwaii.

We had to eat and run because we had a ferry to catch in Prince Rupert, with a chunk of Alberta and the breadth of British Columbia still to cross. Having reduced our luggage to two small bags, we loaded them into the back of Art's jumbo-sized pickup truck, already packed with his bag, a chest freezer, and a generator because what else would one haul to Haida Gwaii?

We drove to Rupert on the Yellowhead Highway, passing through Canada's Banff and Jasper National Parks just west of Calgary. In the daytime, they're two of the most beautiful parks anywhere, but in the dead of night, there wasn't much to see, why the Canadian-nice ranger at the park entrance didn't charge us admission. I'm guessing the freezer in the back convinced her we were only passing through on our way to Haida Gwaii and not sticking around for the scenery.

While there wasn't much to see at the beginning of our trip, Sue did point out, to me, only me, one "historical site" along the way, "There's where I lost my virginity." Good thing she did, point it out, or I would've missed it since Parks Canada didn't deem the site historical marker-worthy.

The three of us took turns driving. It was the first time Sue and I set aside our usual arrangement that when in Canada, she drives, and when in the States, I drive. There were just too many miles to cover in such a short amount of time. Besides, two of us were already exhausted while the other was 78 years old, and we had reservations to keep and many miles to go before we'd sleep, in a bed.

Once through Banff and Jasper, "all" that remained was to drive across British Columbia. For the benefit of those (not you, of course) who still don't know their Canadian geography as well as Alex Trebek thought they should, British Columbia is the size of Texas, Louisiana, and Arkansas combined.

A former colleague, Nigel, from Ireland, once told me how he and his family arrived at the Vancouver airport and decided to spend the day driving around British Columbia to see the sights. I laughed. He laughed. "Back in school, a map of Canada only filled one page in my geography book, so how big could British Columbia be?" As it turned out, eleven times larger than Ireland.

Except to stop for gas, food, bathrooms, and fishing licenses, we drove straight through, arriving in Prince Rupert in the middle of the night. With a few hours to spare before our ferry ride to Haida Gwaii, Art topped off the pickup's gas tank. As expensive as fuel is in Canada, it's even pricier on the islands.

In the wee hours of the morning fog and mist - Rupert the rainiest place in Canada - we made our way to the BC Ferries dock to get in line for the sunrise departure along with hundreds of others in dozens of cars. At 54 degrees north, it was on the cool side, even with the extra hours of sunshine that come in July that far north of the equator.

The 93-nautical mile (107-mile) ferry trip across the Hecate Strait to Haida Gwaii takes seven hours, depending on sea and weather conditions. Because the strait is wide and shallow, the waters can be some of the roughest on the West Coast of North America. While we experienced the vomit-inducing waves of the Hecate Strait on a subsequent crossing - another story for another book - this trip was smooth sailing.

The ferry even had a cafeteria that served a tasty and most welcome breakfast as our road trip snacks began to lose their appeal somewhere around Prince George. The ferry even had a gift shop. I purchased two T-shirts, while Sue snagged a pullover jacket. We still have them, reminding us of a summer we'd never forget, even without the wearable souvenirs.

Around noon, we finally made it to a sunny Haida Gwaii, our ferry docking at Skidegate Landing. Off the boat, we were back on the Yellowhead Highway with still an hour and a half in Art's pickup before we'd arrive in Masset, our final destination, for the time being.

The journey from Dubai to Masset took 72 hours door-to-door, the longest non-stop trip Sue and I have ever taken. I can't imagine a circumstance where we'd make a longer one or agree to, although the destination was well worth the three-day odyssey it took to get there.

While we'd planned our trip to Haida Gwaii months in advance, we hadn't planned on a property off a dead-end dirt road in a remote area of southern Ecuador coming onto our radar less than a month before our scheduled departure from Dubai. We were certain this property, near the small town of Vilcabamba, Ecuador, was exactly the one we'd searched for five years to discover.

008

OUR BOXES WERE GETTING TICKED

After Sue and I made our way from Haida Gwaii to Wisconsin, we were off to Panama. Panama? Yes, Panama, because before we found the property in Ecuador, we found two others there. Early in 2006, we narrowed our property search to Latin America and then narrowed it further to Panama and Ecuador. While our hearts said Ecuador, our heads said Panama. We went with our heads. What were we thinking?

We then narrowed our search in Panama to an area near the border with Costa Rica. Two properties (one owner) we found online caught our eye. While not exactly what we were looking for, they were close, and the asking price more than made up for what wasn't quite right. So even though we'd never been to Panama, we made an offer for both at less than the combined asking price for each.

We then waited for a response… and waited… and waited… and waited… getting our first lesson in Latin American living - paciencia (patience). While we waited for the realtor to respond, we arranged a trip to Panama. If our offer was accepted, we could buy the properties. If not, we could still check out the country before buying another.

"Holy due diligence, Batman! What a concept!"

But as I responded to inquiring Dubai Women's College colleagues over our offer, I found myself comparing Panama to... Dubai. Red flag! Panama had far too much in common with where we wanted to leave. After realizing we were about to trade one boom location for another that was about to, Sue and I agreed to turn our focus to Ecuador and follow our hearts.

We needed some help because, in 2006, virtually no information was available online for prospective property buyers in Ecuador. Only a couple-two-three weeks away from our already planned trip to Haida Gwaii, we emailed the only contact we had in Ecuador, Lee, a writer/editor for a company specializing in expat living. Attached was our one-pager, a document describing the property we were searching for.

After identifying an area of interest, we'd find a local realtor and email them. We'd attach our one-pager with the idea that we wouldn't waste their time on properties that didn't match our search criteria. The problem was that too many realtors had no interest in what we wanted to buy, only in what they wanted to sell - like a condo, in a gated community, next to a golf course, for a million dollars...

"You didn't read our one-pager, did you?"

Even though Lee was not a realtor, he emailed that he just happened to have a property for sale that might interest us, attaching a PDF brochure that was more professional and informative than anything we'd ever received from any realtor in any country. When his email arrived, Sue just happened to be in my apartment. I have no idea why she was there, as her unescorted presence was illegal. Naughty Sue! So, sitting side-by-side, fully clothed, and not touching each other, we read the brochure, together.

With every paragraph, our boxes were getting ticked, and the included photos only heightened our interest. The tension mounted as we neared the end of the brochure because we knew one box had not yet been ticked. Surely, the asking price for such a beautiful property so precisely matching our search criteria would burst our budget and our bubble.

But it didn't.

"YES! YES! YES! Lee read our one-pager!"

We were so excited that it no longer mattered that we hadn't heard from the realtor in Panama, even though a month had passed… and then another… and another… This property near Vilcabamba, Ecuador, had our full attention because we were sure Lee's property was our property.

We just had to figure out how to get there to check it out without changing our round trip to Panama because canceling or changing our flights would prove too costly at such a late date. After some brainstorming, we decided that instead of staying in Panama for three days, we'd travel to Vilcabamba. Sure. Three days. In a country we'd never been. On a continent we'd never been. We can get this done. Sure.

So we added a round-tripper to Ecuador inside our round-tripper to Panama following our trip from Dubai to Haida Gwaii, our bus ride across the Canadian prairie to Minnesota, and then on to Wisconsin. No problem! We arrived at night, as it took us most of the day to get from Wisconsin to Panama. It was much later at night before we finally, finally cleared immigration and customs.

For all the hype Panama got as a great expat destination, Sue and I were not impressed, starting with the Panama City airport. Then, and in the multiple times we've transited there since, we've never seen anyone cleaning anything. Filthy it was. I expected to see chalk outlines around some of the stains on the carpeting and chairs - maybe a warm body. COPA Airlines, Panama's national airline, is pretty good, so we kept transiting there.

Nevertheless, we tried to keep layovers in the Panama City airport (which has since improved after the addition of a new terminal) to a minimum and didn't sit still too long in the terminal lest we end up stuck to our seats, or outlined in chalk. We always brought along something to eat because the airport's "food" court was small, humid, not easily accessible, and the overpriced fare was terrible.

That first time in Panama, we stayed overnight. Not impressed at the airport, we were even less impressed with the hotel and the ride there. Looking back on our first and subsequent trips to Panama, we had no regrets about following our hearts, not our heads, in moving to Ecuador.

The following morning, we took a taxi into downtown Panama City to keep an appointment with a lawyer we'd contacted to handle our potential property purchase. We'd already told her we'd not be buying either of the properties in Panama, but we still wanted to keep our appointment. With a few hours to kill before our flight to Ecuador, why not? Meeting with a lawyer isn't so bad if you have no reason to.

We still had to pay for the hour, but something Rainelda said during our conversation made her fee and our trip to Panama worthwhile. As we chatted in her office, she mentioned that people tend to see the best possible outcome in any opportunity, but lawyers are trained to prepare for the worst, something we would be advised to do.

Good advice it was and still is.

Not all that happy in Panama, our mood changed dramatically as soon as we boarded our midday flight to Quito. After all our travels in July of 2006, we were now just a two-hour flight from Ecuador. And a great flight it was because it was chock-full of Ecuadorians, who took their seat on the plane as if they were making their way to a church pew. They shuffled in, put their stuff away, and sat down. The flight crew didn't even have to prompt them to do so. During the flight, they sat quietly, speaking in hushed tones, if they spoke at all. It's like they were trying not, not to bother their fellow passengers. I half-expected a collection plate to be passed around shortly before landing.

The old Mariscal Sucre International Airport in Quito was right downtown. At an elevation of 9228 feet, landing a jet on the short runway surrounded by buildings and mountains was challenging for the pilot and the passengers, the mountains making for some "interesting" wind currents in the thin air at elevation.

I've been on roller coaster rides that weren't as exhilarating. We rocked and rolled as we circled Quito before the pilot finally triple-bounced us down. Everyone cheered. The kids onboard thought it was the best ride ever! The adults, including Sue and I, were relieved to be safely on the ground. But after the plane parked at the gate, the thrill ride was forgotten, and our fellow passengers disembarked in the same dignified manner they boarded.

On that first flight to Ecuador, the scenery and the locals made a great first impression. We already had a good feeling about Ecuador and its people before we'd even cleared immigration and customs. In contrast to our wait in the dirty and humid Panama City airport, we breezed through the Quito airport's immigration counters, customs check, and exit doors. Almost.

009

IT WAS A DARK AND STORMY NIGHT

Paddling our way from Sunset to Rainbow Lake, we'd only been on Waupaca's Chain O'Lakes for ten minutes when <KA-BOOM> lightning just about obliterated Esther Williams Island, a quarter-acre sandbar dotted with a few trees and a small cabin. "OK, I'm in open water on the top deck of a two-deck steel boat with smokestacks on either side of me…" Before I could finish that thought, before the thunder from the first strike had finished its say <KA-BOOM> lightning struck the even closer Onaway Island, close enough that we saw it in 3D without the headache-inducing glasses.

"Pat, maybe we should head back to the dock."

"Might be a good idea."

With the boat's owner in agreement, I made a literal and figurative hard-to-port turn headed, full speed, back to Taylor Lake and Clear Water Harbor. As we approached, Pat took the helm, giving me a quick lesson on docking the Chief Waupaca, an authentic sternwheel paddleboat. Easing into the slip, just as he brought the boat to a halt by reversing the paddle <KA-BOOM> lightning struck again, and again in 3D, the steel pole supporting a hanging Old Style beer sign the next dock over, lit up.

Somehow, the sign survived, but with the storm showing no sign of letting up - a flagpole at the nearby marina also taking a shot in 3D - Pat figured we wouldn't be going anywhere.

"You might as well go home, John. Come back tomorrow morning at seven-thirty. Patty will tell you what to do."

"OK, Pat," although I had no idea who this Patty was. Next morning, at seven-thirty sharp, I found out after opening the front door to the Harbor Bar & Restaurant, and there, behind the bar's soda dispenser station, stood Patty, pretty as could be, looking like there no place she'd rather be...

"Good morning! You must be John."

Patty's infectious smile made me smile, even though I thought no one should look so good or be so cheery at seven-thirty in the morning. While I was wide-awake the night before, even without the lightning strikes, I was a little foggy my first morning at Clear Water Harbor, where Patty did indeed tell me what to do - clean the bar, restaurant, bathrooms, back bar, back deck, parking lot, and grounds. After I'd finished, she was most impressed with my ability to mop the floor without leaving streaks.

"Wait 'til you see the toilets."

I didn't know it then, but the opening for me was because Patty had traded her captain's hat for an inside job, behind the bar, in front of the grill, at the end of the previous season. After I found out, I thought her crazy to have swapped jobs, even though by then I'd learned the sternwheeler wasn't always easy to pilot with its flat bottom, mere 25-inch draft, and two six-foot rudders mounted behind the paddle.

Patty only told me the tale once, but the day the wind nearly blew the Chief, along with her and her passengers, into the Indian Crossing Bridge, paddle first, was the day I think she decided enough was enough. With her work ethic and positive attitude inspiring me to bring my A-game every day, Patty deserves some credit for my success at Clear Water Harbor. Of course, had she not swapped jobs, I likely never would've had the opportunity to captain the Chief Waupaca.

Thanks also go to Linda, my former Waupaca High School guidance counselor, who, after getting my telephone number from Ma, called to tell me Pat and his wife, Mimi, still at their winter home in the Florida Keys, were looking to hire a new boat captain. Knowing I planned on transferring back to Wisconsin to continue my studies, that my freshman year at the University of Florida would be my last, Linda encouraged me to "Give Pat and Mimi a call."

When I did, Mimi answered the phone. I don't know what Linda told the two, but I got the feeling the job was already mine as Mimi's main concern was, "When can you start?"

"First of May."

"First of May?"

"There's no spring break at the University of Florida - we're already here - so I'm done by the end of April."

"That's great, John. Call us when you get back to Waupaca."

Even over the phone, even though we hadn't met, I could see the smile on her face, as it would be at least mid-May before most Harbor employees would finish their school year. Until then, Pat and Mimi operated their business short-staffed.

Back in Waupaca, I called the Harbor the day before May Day, this time speaking with Pat.

"Can you come down for an interview tonight, around seven-thirty?"

"Seven-thirty? Sure."

Night interview? The hoot-owl in me liked that. Even though Clear Water Harbor was just a ten-minute walk from our house near fabulous downtown King, a "suburb" of Waupaca, I'd never been there. Having never met the man to interview me, I asked a bartender who pointed him out. I then walked over and introduced myself to Mr. Meighan.

"Pat. Call me Pat."

And it was Pat and Mimi from day one. That's the kind of people they were. Their attitude made such an impression on me that never again would I refer to any boss or colleague by anything other than their given name. Except for one obnoxious colleague, as far as I know, no one saw my first-name calling as disrespectful. Instead, it was a not-so-subtle statement of the working relationship I wanted and enjoyed with Pat and Mimi.

Once on a first-name basis, Pat's first words were, "We already hired someone to do the daytime tours, but I think we can find some work for you. We have a three-hour private charter tonight. You up for a boat ride?"

"Sure!"

Fifteen minutes later, I was in the pilothouse of the Chief Waupaca. A bit smaller than a typical office cubicle, it still had eight windows, two doors, and the most bitching steering wheel I'd ever seen - wood, with brass trim, and a good three feet in diameter. After Pat backed the boat out of the dock, much to my surprise, he handed me that wheel, and just like that, I was piloting the Chief.

Even though the Chief was the first motorized boat I'd ever driven, Pat thought that a good thing, telling me experienced drivers had to unlearn what they knew to pilot the sternwheeler, the boat so unlike any other. I scratched my head from the inside over his remark, seeming so improbable I thought he must be trying to boost my confidence.

But years later, bringing the Chief into the dock on a day when the Old Style sign was hanging horizontally in a stiff westerly wind, I spotted a lone man standing on the dock, displaying unusual interest in my landing - there not enough Os in smooth to describe it, I always better with an audience, even of one. After I thanked the debarking passengers, the lone man came over. He introduced himself as a pilot of another (fake) paddleboat that operated on Lake Winnebago and the Fox River, about an hour's drive away.

Pat was looking for someone to pilot the Fall Colors Cruises after I returned to university and asked him to come up for an interview. That interview never happened after the lone man told me, "I don't know how you docked that boat in this wind. Tell Pat there's no way I'm piloting that tub," he then walked away, then drove away. He should've been onboard when I piloted the Chief during a tornado…

While it was a dark and stormy night my first time on the Chief Waupaca, the weather couldn't have been more wrong in foreshadowing my career at Clear Water Harbor. Hired part-time, I never worked it, Pat forced to limit my hours to no more than 48 per week… unless I needed to work more. With so much to do, I added to my job description regularly.

Despite the lightning strikes and my limited time onboard that first night, I knew the opportunity before me was unlike any other. The kind I imagined as a kid when everything was possible, one reason I spent ten seasons, thousands of hours, sitting in the pilothouse's rickety captain's chair, bobbing and weaving with the waves. I might never have left if captaining the Chief Waupaca had been a year-round job that paid more. Thankfully, it wasn't, and it didn't, because even though I would've missed so much had I not gotten the job piloting the Chief, if I'd held it too long, I would've missed so much more.

010

OLD LADY ANTHONY

Living on the corner of Sanctimonious Street and Busybody Boulevard, Old Lady Anthony made no secret of her scorn for that "sinful woman" living across the way, even though, as far as I know, she'd never met my mother. Before Ma and I moved in, Old Lady Anthony demanded the landlord, Eau Claire City Attorney (later City Manager) Ray Wachs, not rent to Ma because she had a child, but <GASP!> no husband. The landlord's wife, Betty, told Old Lady Anthony my mother's references were impeccable and we'd be moving in.

After we did, Old Lady Anthony responded by not allowing her kids to play with me, "that son-of-a... divorcee." Perhaps she was taking cues from her husband, who forbade their children from playing on his precious - the grass around their house. The only person I ever saw walking on the grass was him, and then only behind a push mower.

I understood, as best a child can, why her kids didn't play with me, but I couldn't understand why they never played in their own yard. Then came the day the husband was charged with discharging a firearm within city limits. A neighbor couple called the cops, a couple with an adorable dachshund who loved to play ball with their kids. The ball got away that day, rolling into Old Lady Anthony's yard. Unaware of property lines, the dog ran after the ball to retrieve it, as good dogs do. Old Lady Anthony's husband then shot the dog dead in front of the horrified children.

Not wanting anything to do with such "people," traveling back and forth between our apartment, the school, and Bob and Susie's house, I avoided cutting the corner, Old Lady Anthony's corner, even though it would've cut seconds off my walk. Knowing how she felt about Ma and me, I could've, maybe should've tormented her, cutting that corner with regularity. Instead, I was a good boy and kept my distance.

One summer morning, though, I inexplicably found myself on the sidewalk in front of her house. Oops. Next thing I know, Old Lady Anthony bursts out her front door and starts giving me a lot of lip, insulting me, and then Ma, before her focus turned to my gun, asking more questions than some gun dealers do of potential buyers, questions she apparently never asked her husband. I was only passing by, on a public sidewalk, but Old Lady Anthony just wouldn't shut up. So, as her tongue continued wagging, I raised my rifle, and when the gap between her eyes was in my sights, I pulled the trigger.

<BANG>

That shut her up all right, Old Lady Anthony never speaking to me again...

Fortunately for her, my rifle was just a Daisy Popgun, but with a realistic metal barrel and sound to match, when I fired, she nearly jumped out of her bloomers. Having halted her latest diatribe, and with the rest of my day booked, I continued on my way, knowing Old Lady Anthony couldn't get to her phone fast enough - maybe after a change of bloomers - to let Ma know what a miserable little shit I was.

Sure enough, when Ma and I crossed paths later that day, she asked if I'd done what Old Lady Anthony said I'd done.

"Yes."

"You know you're not supposed to point guns at people, right?"

"Yes."

"And pull the trigger?"

"Yes."

That's it. That's all that happened. Ma didn't ground me. She didn't confiscate my popgun, even though I'm sure she was tempted to because of the loud noise it made, why she forbid me from firing it inside our apartment. Even though it was only a popgun, I know if I'd fired it at anyone else, I would've been in big trouble, but as it was Old Lady Anthony, my admitting I'd done what she said I'd done was the last Ma and I would speak of the incident.

No doubt Old Lady Anthony told anyone who'd listen what that sinful woman's demon seed had done (while conveniently ignoring the despicable deed done by her husband), using my action to justify hers - forbidding her children to play with me. They never did, not even at school, perhaps afraid Mother would spot them from her front stoop. Why, even though I was a "son-of-a... divorcee," living in a dilapidated apartment, one of the neighborhood's poor kids, I felt sorry for hers because they had her for a mother, him for a father, and a well-manicured lawn they could look at, but not touch.

(NOTE: Last I checked, Old Lady Anthony was still alive. Even though I only referred to her in this story as Old Lady Anthony, not by her full name, the same as I did when I was a kid, I still made an effort to change her name because why not? It's been more than half a century. People can change. Well, some people, anyway.

Not that she deserves any protection from her words and deeds, not after how she treated Ma and me. Not that she deserves any more consideration than her now-dead husband showed that dachshund or those neighbor kids. And not that I'm concerned about any legal ramifications - the truth never defamatory, no matter how embarrassing. Nope, it's just that after multiple tries, I stuck with Old Lady Anthony because no other name proved a suitable substitute, even though her maiden name was Dick.)

011

JOHNNY GOT BACK

"Al Ain?"

"Yes."

"It matter how I go?"

"You go any way you want."

"OK. We go Sweihan. New road. No humps."

Living in the United Arab Emirates for only a week, I didn't know there was more than one way to drive between Abu Dhabi and Al Ain, so when my driver asked if I had a preference, I didn't. I really didn't.

My journey to the Abu Dhabi airport cargo terminal and back began with me hanging up on Ma, in anger, the only time I ever recall doing so. She'd just informed me that contrary to my explicit instructions NOT to air freight my belongings from Wisconsin to the United Arab Emirates until I told her to, she went ahead and shipped them anyway.

All the stuff that had not come with me as baggage on my flight the previous week was now on its way, well before I was prepared to deal with it. Barely knowing my way around Al Ain, now I'd have to figure out how to get to Abu Dhabi. Three days later, the need to know was even more urgent after I received a call from the cargo terminal informing me my 17 boxes had arrived.

A chance conversation with Rob, a colleague who'd booked a flight out of Abu Dhabi, helped. With the start of the new school year approaching, Rob had to go, somewhere, the UAE requiring resident expats to leave the country each year, and he had not. Since Rob didn't want to go anywhere, he booked a flight to Manama, Bahrain, a 40-minute puddle jump up the Gulf coast. Underscoring the silliness of it all, he also booked the immediate return flight to Abu Dhabi. He'd be gone less than three hours, but it got him out of the country to get the required exit and entry stamps in his passport.

Still trying to wrap my head around Rob's situation, we agreed to meet at the bus station in downtown Al Ain on Thursday morning (weekends in the UAE Thursday/Friday) at six. From there, he told me we could catch a bus to Abu Dhabi for 10 dirhams ($2.70). To make sure I looked and felt my best for my journey into the unknown, Wednesday (Friday) night, I joined my new neighbors for a night on the town, visiting the only two places in Al Ain where expats could legally purchase alcohol, the pubs in the Hilton and InterContinental Hotels.

Not returning home until two in the morning, I set my alarm for five, knowing I'd never hear it. And I didn't, my internal clock, as usual, giving me a gentle nudge, just enough to wake me in time to shut off the alarm before it went off, saving me a heart-hurting jolt.

After downing a bowl of cereal, toast, and a banana, I found a taxi, a sleepy driver who'd just completed his morning prayers at the neighborhood mosque. Directing him to a bus station I'd only heard about was a challenge, but Rob's directions got me close enough to smell the diesel. Only a week removed from Wisconsin, the walk was thankfully short because even at sunrise, the temperature was already triple digits.

Rob was a short, wiry guy, similar in size to the other passengers on the bus, mostly laborers from the Asian subcontinent who couldn't afford a taxi, much less a car. At six feet tall, I was a relative giant, taller than many UAE residents. My height made it easy for me to see, talk, and reach over almost everyone, especially in crowded queues, but on the bus, my size was a definite disadvantage, the seat rows so close I couldn't sit facing forward. Sitting sideways with my feet in the aisle, I wouldn't get the sleep I'd planned on during the two-hour, 90-mile ride to Abu Dhabi.

Counting speed bumps, what the locals called humps, provided a distraction, as there were 54 of them. 90 miles. 54 humps. Not only did I have to sit sideways, feet in the aisle, away from the windows on a bus with no air conditioning, every hump told me the wheels on the bus go up and down because the shocks on the bus were shot. Not surprising, given the way the driver drove over the humps as if the bus was rigged with a bomb programmed to explode if he didn't maintain a speed of at least 50 mph - a storyline I should've developed because it made for a great movie three years later.

At least the "Reduce Speed Humps Ahead" signs gave me a heads-up before the wheels and passengers on the bus went up and down. Easily amused, I found the signs amusing, especially in the conservative Gulf country, what with the "Humps Ahead" text and the graphic resembling an undone bra, and a black one at that.

Yet, the driver brought the bus to a screeching halt for a car accident on the other side of the divided highway. With the accident having happened hours earlier, all that remained was a brand new Mercedes sedan lying on its side in the median strip, along with a couple of date palms, also lying on their sides, apparently sheared off by the crashing car before losing its forward momentum. Even so, with the driver leading the way, everyone except for Rob and me filed off the bus - the people on the bus get out and gawk, out and gawk, out and gawk…

"What the…?"

"They like accidents," Rob remarked matter-of-factly, without looking up from his book as if he'd seen the scene before.

"How long are we going to be here?"

"Until they've seen all there is to see," Rob remarked matter-of-factly, without looking up from his book as if he'd seen the scene before.

Sure enough, after ten or so minutes, satisfied they wouldn't see any more, or gore, the other passengers filed back on the bus, the driver bringing up the rear. Once everyone was in, we resumed our trip westward, the Abu Dhabi airport and neighboring cargo terminal out in the desert on the way into the city when coming from Al Ain. Not a regular stop, the bus driver dropped me off on the highway, the cargo village a long, hot walk away.

As it was Thursday (Saturday), only a few package pickeruppers like me were milling about customs. A labyrinth of offices, lacking signs that would've told me what each office was for had I been able to read Arabic, I was fortunate to encounter a truck driver looking for work, correctly sensing I had no clue what to do.

"Why you here?"

"To pick up some boxes."

"How many?"

"17."

"Where you go?"

"Al Ain."

"You have truck?"

"No," realizing only then that I had no plan to get my boxes home.

"I have truck. I drive boxes Al Ain."

"…and me?" realizing only then that I had no plan to get me home.

"You want ride?"

"Yes."

"Mafi mushkallah (No problem)."

I was not about to let some stranger load practically everything I owned onto his truck and drive off. He might not go to Al Ain. Given how honest most people were in the UAE, he most assuredly would've driven my boxes to Al Ain, but I didn't know that then. Besides, if I didn't go along for the ride, how could I direct him to my villa, even if I wasn't sure how to get there, and I lived there.

Having agreed he was the man for the job, introductions were in order.

"What your name?"

"John."

"Me, Faisal. American?"

"Yes. Where you from?"

"Pakistan."

Now that we "knew" each other, we agreed on a price. Given we were in a mostly empty airport cargo terminal, and I had no plan or leverage, I agreed to his offer of 250 dirhams (about $70). Later, I would learn that was a fair price - as I said, the UAE was full of honest people, I just didn't know that then. The 250 dirhams included Faisal navigating the bureaucracy on my behalf. That alone was worth the price because even with his help and no queues, it took us half an hour to shuffle from office to office to get the required stamps, seals, and signatures. As all had their separate fee, tagging along with Faisal, I paid 5 dirhams here, 10 dirhams there, and signed John Curran everywhere.

Once the paperwork was complete, Faisal loaded his flatbed truck, overkill for my 17 boxes. After he confirmed our destination and that I had no objection to taking an alternate route, we were on our way to Al Ain, via Sweihan, on the new highway with no humps. A longer drive, but with no humps, it seemed shorter, and despite the temperature pushing 120 degrees, with the windows wide open, the "wind chill" made it feel cooler as long as the truck was moving.

Along the way, Faisal and I chatted about what we saw, but since there wasn't much to see in the middle of nowhere, including other traffic, there wasn't much to chat about. Other than some wandering camels, the only noteworthy thing I saw was an under-construction pipeline running parallel to the highway, a hundred or so yards distant.

"Oil?"

"No, more important. Water."

To break the monotony of the landscape, I shared my brown bag lunch with Faisal. Surprised but grateful for the gesture, he returned the favor by sharing his water. Not sure what to do with my banana peel, Faisal showed me, throwing his out the driver's side window and motioning for me to toss mine, too. Given the arid conditions, it's probably still on the roadside, petrified.

"Sweihan," Faisal announced.

Straddling the newly built highway, the desert oasis wasn't much. In a weird sort of way, Sweihan reminded me of the many two-mile-long, two-block-wide small towns in Wisconsin. All it needed was a railroad track and a grain elevator, as the town already had a water tower. Given my fondness for out-of-the-way places, I saw Sweihan as a glorious and much-appreciated respite for travelers it no doubt was before cars and highways.

Twenty miles later, a left turn at Al Saad put us back on the main highway. With signs informing me Al Ain was just ahead, I could no longer ignore what I had since we left the cargo terminal - the possibility I wouldn't be able to find my way home. Not only were there no street names in Al Ain, but most residential areas looked much the same - block after block of white or off-white two-story villas partly topped by clay-tile roofs.

Knowing not much more than my villa was located in the Al Khabisi sector near the Camel Roundabout, I figured it no time to pretend I knew where I was going. So I let Faisal know I wasn't sure how to get to my villa - you know, coming from Abu Dhabi, but from anywhere else I could find it. Sure, I could. He appeared perplexed until I explained I'd just moved to Al Ain the previous week.

"We need to find the Camel Roundabout. From there, I know the way."

Yet to see anything familiar since entering the city limits, roundabout-by-roundabout, my anxiety grew. I want to say I knew all along the Camel Roundabout was on the road from Abu Dhabi, but it was just dumb luck. Happy as I'd been since hanging up on Ma, with the exuberance of a man who'd just won the lottery, because I had, I pointed to the topiary camel ahead, "Left at the roundabout!"

A legal U-turn, a right, a right, a left, and a right turn later, Faisal parked his truck in front of my villa. He even helped me unload my boxes and carry them inside, no charge. I paid him extra anyway, also throwing in a bottle of cold water after we settled the bill. Following a hearty handshake, he drove away, leaving me standing in the blazing midday sun, shaking my head in disbelief as I conducted a third-person review of my morning.

"You were out late with your friends. You had maybe two hours of sleep. You barely knew where you were going. You had no idea what to do when you got there. You had no plan for getting your boxes or yourself to Al Ain. You weren't even sure you could find your way home. But you got back, with your boxes, and, and, you've been to Sweihan."

012

A SENSE OF HUMOR

A toolbox. Of everything you might guess I packed in July 1991 as I prepared for my first move to the United Arab Emirates, my toolbox probably wouldn't make your top ten, but something told me I'd need mine. And I did, almost immediately, because my villa required some work, little things, but impossible without the proper tools, like those in my trusty toolbox, one I made in a high school shop class.

But even before I left for the UAE, clearing numerous paperwork hurdles to get a made obsolete before I arrived entry visa taught me there was a tool I'd rely on more than any other moving to, then living in, a country and culture far different from mine. Yet, it was not in my toolbox but in me - a sense of humor. Helpful as it was preparing to move to the UAE and then living there, a sense of humor was an absolute necessity once Sue and I began our preparations to move from one foreign country to another.

We can laugh, now, over the paperwork required just to get our three cats out of the UAE and into Ecuador. I never saw so many stamps, seals, and signatures on three pieces of paper, the documents Louvre-worthy works of art ideally suited for the

Rococo section. After we arrived in Quito, I pleaded with a customs agent to let me keep that paperwork, but he refused, and I didn't think to take any photos.

One reason for the excess of stamps, seals, and signatures on all our documents was our unusual circumstances - two English speakers moving from an Arabic-speaking country to a Spanish-speaking country, along with geography, the nearest Ecuadorian consulate in Cairo. Cairo, Egypt. Egypt. On another continent. And that the Ecuadorian consulate required all our Emirati documents to be authenticated at the Egyptian Consulate in Dubai. If you think about it, with your head in a vice, it makes perfect sense.

So before we ever dealt with Latin American bureaucracy, we had to deal with not one but two layers of Arab bureaucracy. In addition, we had to get all our documents translated from Arabic to English and then to Spanish, as the Ecuadorian Consulate, for reasons they never made clear, would not permit direct translation from Arabic to Spanish. At each of the many steps along the way, our documents collected another stamp, seal, and signature as those handing us the documents collected fees from Sue and me.

While the cats required more paperwork than we did, Sue and I still had to visit a police station in the emirate issuing our residence visas - Sharjah for Sue, Dubai for me - to get clearance letters stating we had no criminal record. For the first time, police fingerprinted me. As for Sue? I can't say... Then, shortly after we arrived in Ecuador, we were fingerprinted again, our thumbprints laminated on our cedulas, Ecuador's national ID card.

Then came moving day. With a 20-foot container (another story for another book) already hauled away two weeks previous, we were cruising before we were flying. Our bags were packed, and the cat carriers were ready to go - ticket labels, name tags, vaccination tags, and special instructions (Tissa'a could be lethal, Iqqy was blind, and Bubbuh was... Bubbuh) all attached or affixed. I even baked dozens of cookies so we'd have something to eat along the way and at our new home, knowing we'd find the cupboards bare and the fridge unplugged.

Sue and I sat on the floor in my virtually empty apartment overlooking Sharjah's Qasbah Canal on the evening of our departure. Waiting... waiting...

I got so bored that I finally read the fine print on my airline ticket.

"SUE!"

We quickly repacked our bags, knowing we were still screwed, especially with three cats to check along with our suitcases. We left behind a few things to reduce weight, including most of the cookies we'd baked, gifting them to our delighted taxi driver, Ramadan, who drove us from Sharjah to the Dubai airport. He thought we were being nice, grateful for his services over the years, and we were, not six-dozen cookies worth maybe, but I wasn't going to tell him how much those cookies would cost us when we checked in.

Despite our manic repacking, a sense of humor came in handy on July 14th, 2007, when a KLM Royal Dutch Airlines agent working the check-in counter at the Dubai airport presented us with an excess baggage charge of $1800. $1800. Sure, our three cats were flying with us, but the majority of that bill was the result of our travel agent in Dubai failing to mention (and I failing to notice until that evening) that our combined baggage allowance was only 88 pounds, not even two bag's worth, even by today's lowered limit.

The KLM agent thought there must be some mistake, why he checked. Then double-checked. Then checked again. He even called over his manager to make sure there was no mistake. That manager then called over their manager. There was no mistake. $1800 it was. $1800. The agent apologized profusely as he collected most of the cash we'd planned on living on until we got set up in Ecuador. The experience made it easier to say "Adios!" to the Emirates and travel agents.

In hindsight, we could've used that $1800 to buy business class tickets from Dubai to Quito with a much bigger baggage allowance. We might not have saved any money, but at least we would've flown in style for most of our 50-hour, yes, 50-hour journey from Dubai to Vilcabamba… with our cookies. If not for the snafu, we would've escaped the UAE with only minor bumps and bruises. Instead, we left with a nasty $1800 scar that has faded over time.

Not arriving at our new home near Vilcabamba until after dark, we set up the cats with food, water, and a litter box and then went to bed, bodies beyond tired, minds beyond frazzled. So you can imagine my delight when Day 1 in our new home began with me waking up to find the water supply pipe to the bathroom sink spent the night taking a leak all over the floor.

There was just one pipe because the only hot water available on our property was in the main house and guesthouse showers, courtesy of ten-dollar El Cheapo brand electric on-demand water heaters mounted on the shower head. To work, those "heaters" required flipping a "Frankenstein switch," the kind that's fried a few showering residents of Ecuador.

We still had water, so not so bad, but after dealing with the leaky pipe, a short time later, when I tried to connect the gas cylinder to the stove that came with the house, the fitting fell off, rusted to dust. I shouldn't have been surprised, given it was an open-air kitchen in a location that receives a fair bit of rain and the stove an El Cheapo brand.

At least the house came with a modest brick barbecue that more resembled a fireplace, our only means to cook until we went to town, returning with a two-burner gas hotplate. We could've purchased a replacement stove, but we didn't, not with our 40-inch, five-burner Whirlpool packed in a shipping container sailing somewhere on the Indian Ocean between Dubai and Guangzhou, China.

That first morning in Ecuador, after dealing with the leaky pipe and the rusted stove fitting, karma rewarded us with the discovery of an unknown backyard water feature. While it lacked the scale and splendor of the fountains fronting the Bellagio in Las Vegas, it was still a good show, considering we were on a mountainside in a remote part of southern Ecuador, far from the bright lights of anywhere.

Upon inspection, I discovered the "fountain" sprang from a buried water pipe. I'd never seen a break like that, the metal cracked right down the middle of the El Cheapo brand valve. You'd think (we did) that shutting off the water from the storage tank, atop a concrete platform, atop a concrete column, filled by a submerged pump in a ten-foot deep hand-dug well on our lower property would've put a stop to the fountain, same as it did to the leaky bathroom pipe, but it didn't.

"So where is this water coming from?"

Later, there were more puzzlers…

"Why did the water stop?"

"Will it ever come back?"

"And if so, when?"

Weeks later, we learned from a neighbor that our mystery water came from the cabrada (ravine) two lots over via a plastic pipe buried under the dirt road. Whenever water flowed down the cabrada, our backyard looked a little like the Bellagio until I replaced the fractured valve with the help of the tools in my toolbox and the one in me - a sense of humor.

I needed it because when we went to bed after the first full day in our new home off a dead-end dirt road, we were down to one working light bulb. One.

<POP>

None. We were down to none.

Now, on Day 2…

013

YOU KICK ANY WAY YOU WANT

"What did you do?"

"I punted a ball onto the roof."

"A first-grader?"

"Yeah! A first-grader!"

As Principal of Longfellow Elementary on Eau Claire's near north side, the man with the Johnny Unitas buzzcut seemed more impressed than upset one of his school's younger pupils punted a ball onto the roof, but then Mr. Deniston had a different way of looking at things. That's why I liked him, never minding my time in his office over things others claimed I'd done.

New to the job, he seemed to know what he was doing and demonstrated as much after I punted a kickball onto the roof to see if I could. I could. The school was three stories tall. I was seven years old. Unfortunately, my former kindergarten teacher, Miss Rogstad, witnessed my "crime" while on recess patrol.

"John! Mr. Deniston's office. Now!"

"...no wonder it's Miss Rogstad," I muttered to myself as I made my way to Mr. Deniston's office. Once seated in front of the man behind the desk, I had no idea how much trouble I was in and didn't want to find out. Hoping to change the subject of our conversation from my crime and punishment to anything else, I pointed at a framed photo on the wall behind Mr. Deniston.

"Who's that guy?"

"President Nixon."

"Oh... does he always look like that?"

We talked some, just chitchat, without mentioning what I'd done. After Mr. Deniston decided I'd been punished enough, he sent me back to class. As I went out the door, he half asked, half told me, "John, no more balls on the roof, OK?"

"OK." Respect.

If only I could've punted Miss Rogstad onto the roof, no one would've found her until summer when firefighters used the school building for training. With the aid of their ladder truck, they'd climb over the parapet wall and onto the school's flat roof, tossing down whatever they found up there - kickballs, Frisbees, kindergarten teachers - to anxiously awaiting kids. If summer vacation wasn't already fabulous enough, I got fire trucks, firefighters, and a shot at free stuff that day.

From kindergarteners to fifth graders, there were hundreds of students at Longfellow Elementary. Shoe-horned onto a city block otherwise full of single-family homes in a blue-collar neighborhood featuring a factory, the school didn't have much playground space. Why, at recess, most kids leaned against the chain-link fence and watched the older kids play - kickball the game, even in the snow.

Older boys monopolized the two teams comprised of nine or ten players a side, the game, more or less, played by the same rules as baseball. Every now and then, I'd convince them to give me a chance, but after another feeble attempt to send the ball flying, they'd banish me to the chain-link fence with the rest of my classmates. I could punt a ball onto the roof but couldn't kick one out of the infield to earn a place on a team.

Like everyone, I kicked straight on, like American football kickers did, contacting the ball first with the toe of the shoe. Kicking in football was not pretty then, the job too often done by a chunky guy wearing a black square-toed shoe on his kicking foot. Then I saw a game on TV involving the Kansas City Chiefs and their kicker, Jan Stenerud, who changed my "approach" to kicking a football.

From Norway, Stenerud attended Montana State University on a ski-jumping scholarship. One day, the university's head basketball coach noticed his kicking ability and informed the head football coach, who suggested Stenerud try American football. He did, achieving a rare double in American university athletics - named an All-American in football and ski jumping. His professional career, in football, led to Stenerud's induction into the National Football League's Hall of Fame, a first for a pure kicker.

The TV announcers referred to Stenerud and others like him as soccer-style kickers. They so revolutionized American football that announcers would refer to them as kickers in less than a generation. I don't remember when the transformation was complete, but "When was the last time a network play-by-play announcer described a kicker as soccer-style?" would make for a tremendously tough trivia question.

While Stenerud wasn't the first soccer-style kicker in pro football, he was the first to demonstrate the superiority of taking a different approach to the ball. During his first three seasons with Kansas City, he made

70% of his field goals, compared with a 53% average for other pro kickers. The league was soon flooded with soccer-style kickers, many foreign-born, often with names containing an overabundance of consonants.

In contrast to straight-on kickers, #3 for the Chiefs kicked with style (easier to do without the clunky square-toed shoe) and power (he got a longer leg swing into the ball). The sideways approach appeared more fluid and natural, so I tried it with my football in the backyard of our apartment. After my first attempt, the Chiefs became my favorite NFL team, and Jan Stenerud my favorite player. I even wrote a letter to the Kansas City Chiefs asking if they could send me some "KC" decals for my red football helmet. Head Coach Hank Stram responded, sending the decals and a handwritten thank you note for being a Chiefs fan in Wisconsin.

Now armed with a new approach to kicking, I pleaded my way into another kickball game, "I've been practicing!" Waiting for the pitch, I stood off to the side of home plate instead of behind it. With the pitcher delivering the ball toward me, not home plate, I bent over and scooped it up.

"What are you doing?" some sneered.

Ignoring their remarks, I threw the ball back to the pitcher, asking him to aim for home plate, not me. <BOOM> The ball flew off the side of my foot, I finally getting to do something I'd never done before - run the bases, all the bases.

The big kids that had moved in learned they needed to move back, and I no longer suffered the indignity of fielders moving in. And no longer would I lean on the chain-link fence during recess because with that one kick, what grade I was in, or how big I wasn't no longer mattered, only that I was good. There's a life lesson there.

I became something of a hero to the younger kids on the playground as one of their own was now in the game. One girl, probably sweet on me, liked to give the older kids the business, reminding them from the chain-link fence that a second-grader could kick as well, if not better than they could. Behind every successful boy, there's a girl, mocking his peers. These days, I'm sure she's making some man very happy.

My time at Longfellow ended during the summer between second and third grade when Ma got her first teaching job. I had to leave behind the neighborhood, school, and friends. Since my number one fan didn't live nearby, I never got to say goodbye. I have a mental image of her leaning against the fence the following school year, watching the kickball games, wondering where that no-account boy went.

To Waupaca, where in my new neighborhood, there was no school, no playground, there wasn't even a town, our rental home just outside the city limits, on Lawson Drive, 15 one-story three-bedroom houses lining the dead-end dirt (we aspired to gravel) road. The entrance was off Highway 54, sandwiched between Wendt Motors, a Ford dealership, and a single-family home owned by a county employee who plowed our road after it snowed.

Lawson Drive ended at a planted pine forest high above the Waupaca River. Behind the car dealership was a farm field, the half closest to Lawson Drive forever fallow. On the opposite side was Faulks Brothers, a construction company, enticing the kids in the 'hood with mini-mountains of sand, rocks, gravel, and dirt.

Living just outside the east side of town, my new school, Westwood Elementary, was not only in town, it was across town, on the... yes, the west side. How did you know? I was shocked at the small size of my new school after stepping off the bus on my first day. In contrast to Longfellow, Westwood was just one story, just six classrooms - two each for grades three to five. In addition to a few support rooms, there was also a "cafegymatorium," the amalgamation a little too much of each and not enough of either. Outside, the playground wasn't much larger than the footprint of the school building.

Westwood had a few things working in its favor, however. One, kickball was the game. Two, many of my classmates and I are still friends. And three, my teacher was Mrs. Jome. That dear woman was one of the best teachers I ever had, and with 37 years of experience in school - 22 as a student and 15 as a teacher - I know a little about good and bad teachers. What kind of teacher was Mrs. Jome? The kind who encouraged my friends and me to continue drawing pictures of penguins we'd seen in a *Ranger Rick's* magazine - we drawing those birds wearing football uniforms - and then posting our works of art in her classroom as if they were Louvre-worthy.

Same as at Longfellow, the other students at Westwood kicked straight-on, so my first time up, I again had to instruct the pitcher to deliver the ball toward home plate, not me. Like the older boys at Longfellow, after I demonstrated my new approach to kicking, my classmates at Westwood learned they needed to move back, But no matter how far back they stood, I just kicked the ball over their heads.

When a couple of classmates moved back to the chain link fence separating the playground from Morton Street, I kicked the ball over the fence, the equivalent, in my estimation anyway, of kicking a ball onto the roof at Longfellow. Why I was always the first one picked when choosing sides for teams. As the new kid, what more could I ask for? Kickball got me off to a good start in a new school and with my new classmates.

Except for one. There's always one, isn't there? Apparently, he never ended up on my team because he got progressively frustrated with my success. He even tried to get the other kids to change the rules of the game so that if I kicked the ball over everyone's head, I'd be out. To their credit, my classmates refused to go along with his evil scheme. After his frustration finally got the best of him, resulting in a playground meltdown, he complained to an adult, our teacher, Mrs. Jome.

He insisted I shouldn't be able to kick the way I did because "It's wrong! It's not fair!" And that I should have to kick straight-on like everyone else. The excellent teacher she was, Mrs. Jome listened to my classmate's complaint - he entitled to his opinion, no matter how stupid it was. A minute or so later, after emptying his brain, Mrs. Jome told him he should be a good sport, find another game if he didn't like how I kicked, or try kicking my way.

That was the last time he complained about me, my kicking anyway. While he never said so, I think part of his problem with me was that he was the tallest kid in class until I came along, and from what I could tell, he didn't have anything else going for him. After he left our conversation, Mrs. Jome, sensing I was still upset, said seven words that have stuck with me to this day: "John, you kick any way you want."

There's a life lesson there too.

014

LOSE YOUR ASS-WIPING MIND

"You're probably wondering how my ass is doing."

How's that for creating some social distancing? During a pandemic, if you want to create some social distancing, with Americans anyway, talk about bidets and build them up as the greatest invention since the flush toilet, because Americans won't want to hear about it. Not one word.

Americans love their toilet paper so much that what did they do after realizing there was a global pandemic? They hoarded toilet paper. What did our Ecuadorian neighbors do? They stocked up on rice, potatoes, and onions. Think about that next time you're sitting on a toilet.

Even though Americans love their toilet paper, they don't like to talk about it, or anyone else to talk about it, not what you do with it anyway. On TV, there was Miss Flagg, aka Charlotte Rae, aka Mrs. Garrett (you take the good, you take the bad, you take them both, and there you have the facts of life), taking no responsibility for her actions, claiming Charmin "So squeezably soft, it's irresistible!"

Before that, Mr. Whipple was lurking in supermarket aisles, ready to scold customers with his iconic line, "Please don't squeeze the Charmin." If you didn't know better, you might think this Charmin was a fluffy bunny. Try wiping your ass with one. Tell me how that goes.

I was too young to remember or be aware, but given the TV ads that ran during my childhood, squeezing rolls of toilet paper must've been a thing, like not wearing a seat belt, smoking while pregnant, or dropping acid. Squeezing toilet paper rolls might seem like a victimless crime, but Madison Avenue apparently felt there was sufficient need for an ad campaign to stop the practice. If that's what the Mad Men were up to, it worked because I've seen a lot of life in supermarket aisles, but never have I seen anyone squeezing rolls of toilet paper. Never.

Ads on American TV are somewhat better these days, inching ever closer to telling the truth about toilet paper's actual purpose. They've still got a ways to go, though, what with ads for Charmin featuring bears, talking, cartoon, bears discussing Junior's sporty red with white trim underwear lying on the bathroom floor, and, "Eew!" who will pick it up?

"Not me!"

Exactly. And why don't the loving parents want to pick up Junior's underwear? While Papa Bear and Mama Bear discuss the subject obliquely, I have two words for you - skid marks. Of course, the new and improved version promises "Charmin Clean," the best-known maker of American toilet paper finally admitting its product hasn't been getting the job done.

Nevertheless, as the pandemic became a thing, some Americans purchased enough toilet paper to last a lifetime, particularly if they caught a fatal case of COVID-19 doing so. All that hoarding did was create the problem they feared - a toilet paper shortage.

To which too many would respond, "I don't care, I got mine."

"Well, so do I. A white porcelain fixture, right next to the toilet."

One of the benefits of living where I've been since 1991 is that I haven't owed, so I haven't paid income tax to any government. With the hope that you don't need a chiropractor to treat the whiplash you just suffered, I'll continue... Here's another thing I haven't done since 1991: I haven't purchased toilet paper, not for myself, not one stinking roll. I didn't need to because my villa in Al Ain had two bidets, as did my first apartment in Sharjah, while my second had, count along with me, "One, two, three! Three bidets!"

Bidets were common in the United Arab Emirates. I never saw a villa or apartment that didn't have at least one. Even in public restrooms, where bidets were not practical, a spray hose - a suitable substitute - was often attached to the wall next to the toilet.

After my enlightenment regarding bidets, that they were so foreign to Americans struck me as odd, given my country's reputation for having the world's best plumbing. Maybe not the best fixtures, though, at least not a complete set. But before I learned to appreciate bidets, I admit I, too, made them the butt of jokes.

Bidets were the easiest targets, mainly since most of the crowd I hung with, including me, had never seen one, much less used one. That and they were so... un-American... a French thing, the word bidet, French for a pony, as a user rode one like a pony. Now, isn't that adorable? But the responses to the mere suggestion of using a bidet ranged from "Eew!" to "Gross!"

Years of experience riding a bidet like a pony later, I would ask, "Gross as wiping your ass with paper mâché?" Do you grab a roll of Charmin to clean yourself when you're dirty and sweaty after a hard day's work?   No, you jump in the shower, where running water, soap, and scrubbing do the job. When you're done, I venture your ass is far cleaner than it ever is after a paper wipe.

Why, when we remodeled our house near Vilcabamba, I installed a bidet. One, but then in a world with no toilet paper, even the man with but one bidet is king. I appreciate our bidet even more in Ecuador, where it's common to see signs posted in bathrooms, public and private, reminding users to drop their used toilet paper into the trash.

"Eeew!"

"Gross!"

The reason for this is that plumbing in Ecuador rarely meets American standards, and many septic systems are incapable of handling the extra load. The throwing instead of flushing often causes some degree of consternation among newbies from North America not used to South American "customs." It wouldn't surprise me to learn some expats moved back because they were unwilling, for the rest of their lives, to throw away rather than flush away their toilet paper.

In rural areas, the best septic systems are often no more than cesspools - underground holding tanks to store raw sewage until it breaks down. Three meters across and probably two deep, ours is the largest I've seen, but then our property was once a weekend getaway for a former mayor of Loja, and you know how full of shit some politicians are.

Even if I hadn't installed a bidet in our house, throwing toilet paper into the trash instead of the toilet wouldn't have been an issue, as I spent ten years piloting the Chief Waupaca. For in each of the sternwheel paddleboat's two claustrophobic restrooms, there was a sign asking users, "Please Do Not Put Anything Into The Head Unless You Have Eaten It First," because anything other than bodily waste filled the toilets and the septic tank they drained into more rapidly than necessary. Worse, and I know, I know, foreign objects clogged and often ruined the impeller in the pump I used to drain the septic tank. Oh, I wished anyone who ever told me mine was a cushy job would've been around for one of those character-building episodes.

But with a bidet, I don't need to throw away toilet paper, buy any, or hoard it in a crisis. For a bidet to work, all that's required is running water. If I don't have that, I have far more severe problems than a dirty bum. For one, I can't flush. So it was with some amusement that I watched Americans lose their ass-wiping minds buying all the toilet paper they could.

Some prejudiced against the bidet claim that they waste water. Yet nearly two pounds of wood and more than six gallons of water are needed to produce one roll of toilet paper, and that's not counting the gallons of water the tree consumed before it was cut. That's why I didn't feel guilty about the fraction of a gallon of water required for each use of our bidet, water collected in a mountain pool in the nearby Podocarpus National Park, piped to our house pretty much as is. Water that flowed through our bidet, to the cesspool, then into the soil, watering, perhaps fertilizing our huilco trees. That's the waste from a bidet. Now compare that to all that toilet paper.

Researchers in Japan, home to some of the world's most high-tech bathroom appliances, asked 32 nursing students to wear clean medical gloves when doing their number 2s. What are students for? Examining those gloves afterward, those researchers found more than 40,000 different viable bacteria attached to them, while the bacteria attached to the gloves of bidet users was little more than a tenth of that.

If you're still squeezing your toilet paper rolls, I offer this story to bolster my case... On our way to Green Bay's Lambeau Field for a Packers game, I sat in the backseat of my best friend Dan's SUV, his older brother, Jim, riding shotgun. One thing I enjoyed about our road trips, even though Green Bay was only an hour away, was that the subject of conversation could be just about anything. Anything...

On this ride, or at least for a part of it, the subject was a waitress at Waupaca's Oakwood Restaurant who shall remain nameless for reasons that will soon become apparent. The night before, after the restaurant had closed, Jimmy told of chatting her up at the Oakwood's bar. After knocking back a few cold ones, she told Jim she'd showered in preparation for her shift at the restaurant, only to realize she had to poop as she headed out the door.

"I was late for work because after I pooped, I had to take another shower."

She knew. She knew! That waitress knew the truth about toilet paper - that it doesn't get the job done. If she'd had a bidet, she wouldn't have felt the need to take another shower, well, not a full one anyway, and maybe she would've made it to work on time.

Still not convinced? Have you ever changed a diaper? Did you wipe the baby's butt with toilet paper? No? Because paper only moves shit, it doesn't remove it. I changed a few diapers in my day, and that day was years before I rode a porcelain pony. Even so, if there'd been a suitable bathroom - tiled floors and walls with floor drains - common sense would've had me holding up that baby and then hosing them down.

"No, I never had children. Why do you ask?"

Besides the bidets, the villa and two apartments I called home in the UAE had such bathrooms. How convenient, because with a shower head on a hose and/or a spray hose mounted to the wall, cleaning my bathrooms was easy. Fun even as I'd spray water all over the place, the effect making me feel like I was in a submarine damaged by depth charges <sigh> I miss the comic strip *Calvin and Hobbes*.

Before beginning my assault on bathroom germs, I only needed to remove anything I didn't want to get wet, like towels. Towels get wet as they dry. English is weird. And toilet paper, yes, toilet paper would've been removed if there'd been any. I then cleaned my bathrooms, but not with toilet paper. Instead, I sprayed, soaped, scrubbed, and rinsed them clean.

Just like my bum.

015

MENS NOT ALLOWED

"Jama Banat."
    "Jama Islami."
    "Jama Banat."
    "Jama Islami."
    "Jama… Banat," I insisted, again, uttering those Arabic words with the confidence of someone who'd lived in the United Arab Emirates for years, not the days I had. Until I got a car, that's how it went my first few weeks in Al Ain, Pakistani taxi drivers taking me where they thought I should go, Jama Islami (UAE University Men's Campus), not where I wanted to go, Jama Banat (Women's Campus).

    I'm sure the taxi drivers thought they were doing me a favor because many believed "mens" were not allowed at Jama Banat. Therefore, I must have been mistaken in asking them to take me there, seeing how I was one of those "mens" - a Westerner who didn't know better. Why, despite my insistence, my taxi driver drove me to the Men's Campus, announcing upon arrival, "Jama Islami" as if I didn't know where I was. Not getting out of his taxi nor reaching for my wallet to pay the fare, his frustration was showing and growing, as was mine.

"Jama… Banat."

"No! No! No! Mens not allowed!"

"Mafi… Mushkallah. Jama… Banat."

After venting some of his frustration on the taxi's gearshift, and then the gas pedal, we zoomed off to Jama Banat, or the nearest police station. I wasn't sure which until he'd driven most of the way to the Women's Campus along the city's beautifully landscaped boulevards, date palms lining the sides and filling the medians.

I don't know if my use of the Arabic phrase "mafi mushkallah" (no problem) convinced him I knew better, or he thought the only way he'd collect a fare and get me out of his taxi was to take me where I wanted to go. Maybe both. Maybe it was my frustration showing and growing.

With both driver and passenger highly agitated, we spoke not a word during the five-mile drive from downtown Al Ain to Jama Banat, the barbed wire-topped concrete wall surrounding the campus adding to its intrigue. Why, while taking taxis to and from the Women's Campus, located on a sunken flat on the outskirts of the city, more often than not, I observed drivers not watching the road, instead craning their necks to see what there was to see on the forbidden side of the wall.

"Jama Banat," he declared after stopping in the turnaround just outside the main gate - taxi drivers definitely included in the "mens" not allowed on the Women's Campus. Handing him the fare, my "Shukran" was sarcastic, thanking him for finally taking me where I wanted to go. After extricating myself from his tiny Toyota, the taxi driver waited, confident I'd soon need a ride back to Jama Islami, and he was no doubt dying to get in an "I told you so."

If that's what he was waiting for, he was disappointed. I was smiling and waving, his jaw agape, as I walked through the main gate, past security, backward. He then drove away with a story to tell his fellow taxi drivers. However, something tells me that no matter how convincing his storytelling, his colleagues never would've believed him, claiming, "No! No! No! Mens not allowed!" except for any who'd already given me a ride to Jama Banat after taking me to Jama Islami.

016

417 1/2 McDONOUGH STREET

Built in 1871 for a well-to-do family, the nails holding the house together were square-cut and made of iron, rusted iron. A subsequent owner divided the house into four two-bedroom apartments - two up and two down on the north and south ends. By 1963, when Ma and I moved into the south-end upstairs apartment, the once grand home was affordable housing for the poor, the rent just $50 a month.

Set slightly above the bottom slope of Mt. Tom, Eau Claire's highest point, in its day, the front porch would've provided a commanding view west across the flatland on the city's north side. To the north was Dell's Pond, the old log reservoir, more or less a product of the dam across the Chippewa River next to the paper mill to the west. To the south was the drop-off to the Eau Claire River, where factories produced batteries, tires, and bread, my old neighborhood an interesting mix of smells.

With the entries to the downstairs apartments off the front porch, what little yard fronting the house "belonged" to those tenants, so I stayed off. One morning, though, I wandered onto the grass after spotting a "fortune" in one and five-dollar bills scattered about. When I showed Ma the money I'd found, poor as we were, she told me to put it back as it wasn't ours, and the downstairs neighbors needed it more.

The only other front yard experience I recall was the summer night Ma rousted me from bed in my jammies so Grandma Curran could take a picture of me with Dr. Clay Curran. Living in Lead, South Dakota, research into his family tree led him to Grandpa and Grandma Curran in Elk Creek, who drove him to Eau Claire to meet Ma and me.

In his write-up, he described me as their sturdy grandson, a product of a broken marriage between high school sweethearts. A few years later, when Grandpa and Grandma drove me to South Dakota to see the sights - the Badlands, Mount Rushmore, Crazy Horse Memorial, Deadwood, and, and, the Corn Palace - we also visited Dr. Curran and his wife, in Lead, not the Corn Palace.

A narrow concrete walk on the south side of the apartment house led to a flight of covered wooden stairs added to the back of the building. Apparently, the builder didn't do much planning as the top of the stairs ended a couple of steps short of our door, so the last step was three times the normal height. Despite the large pane of glass in the top half of the door, we couldn't tell who was knocking unless the knockers were reasonably tall.

When I was a tike, I could climb the stairs, but that last step was too tall after almost reaching the top. So I'd reach in and grab the leg of a chair parked at the kitchen table - one of those metal pole frame jobs with nothing more than fiberboard and a bit of padding for the back and bum - and pull myself up. Then came the day I weighed more than the chair, so instead of pulling myself up and in, I pulled the chair out and down.

Of all the things I remember, that would be memory Number 1.

The spindly chair and I made quite a racket as we tumbled down the stairs before rolling onto the concrete step at the bottom. Landing on my back with my bleeding head turned to the left, I saw our neighbor, Doris. After hearing the commotion in the stairway, she came running up the walk. Ma was in her bedroom changing clothes when she heard what Doris heard, and like our neighbor, also came running, down the stairs, in her underwear. Once she determined I was more or less OK, she hoped not every neighbor noticed, especially Old Lady Anthony.

Around back, another stairway led to the basement, I parking my bike on a ledge at the top. In all the years we lived there, the only time I went down those stairs was the day we moved out, I discovering the walls rock, the floor dirt, the spiders many, and an old carom board with a complete set of playing pieces I still have. Also out back, off our kitchen/dining area, was an added-on and enclosed porch with new aluminum storm windows that looked out of place in a house built six years after Abraham Lincoln's assassination.

Covered with charcoal-colored asphalt shingles, the apartment house looked like a roof gone sideways. Those shingles soaked up the sun's rays in the summer, turning our second-floor south-side apartment into a sweat box. The first time I watched the movie *The Bridge on the River Kwai*, after Japanese captors punished the English commander by placing him in a sheet metal box under the tropical Burmese sun, I told the TV, "Still better than a hot summer day in our apartment on McDonough Street!"

To help with the heat, we had an electric fan, a 30-inch model made of metal back in the day when such things were not made of plastic - a fan Ma still has because it still works. On hot nights, she'd set the fan in my bedroom door, facing in, tacking a blanket above to close off the rest of the airflow so the fan would force the hot air out my window, lowering the temperature in my room one, maybe two degrees. On such nights, if I fell asleep on my back, the burning sensation from the sweat pooling in my eyes would wake me up.

Upstairs, in a house without insulation, we could feel the heat rising through the floor. But in the winter, that was a good thing, as the only other heat source was in the living room, an old rust-colored gas space heater, slightly larger than my Uncle David's 1957 Renault Dauphine he purchased for $100. My first spoken word, taught me by Grandma Curran, was "hot," both a warning and a reason for staying away from the heater. Ma shuddered every time its pilot light went out, knowing she'd have to light it, she perhaps hearing stories of explosions, flying body parts…

While the heater was hot, the space not heater-adjacent was not, partly because the apartment was drafty. In the winter, the wind chill near the single-pane windows - often frosted, thanks to condensation - made the apartment feel even colder. With all that dry air seeping in, one winter night, without warning, a blood vessel in my nose cracked and burst. I felt like I was drowning, blood gushing out my nose, yet somehow, not a drop spilled on the white cotton bedspread. The doctor said I was lucky not to bleed to death, which is why he strongly recommended Ma get a humidifier, which she did, my nose never again bubbling blood… because of dry air.

Squeezed between the kitchen and back porch was the one small bathroom. Before Ma got a through-the-window air conditioner for her bedroom, on hot summer nights, she sometimes slept in the white clawfoot bathtub, the sink and toilet too small. Resting on top of the toilet tank was a metal shelving unit Ma bought from K-mart and put together all by herself. So proud of her effort, only on moving day did family finally tell her the shelving had been upside down all along. I thought it worked better that way.

The bathroom opened onto the room that was the kitchen and dining area. With the refrigerator tucked in the corner, the only counter space was a bit between it and the gas stove and on either side of the sink. Next to the sink sat a big drinking glass, iridescent green with a crystalline pattern and texture. A gift from my Great-Grandma Henry, it was easily the prettiest thing in the kitchen. And get this… at any time, I could use that glass to help myself to as much water as I wanted because if Ma ever asked, "What do you want to drink?" and then fetched it for me, I don't recall.

With the house no longer on the level, assuming it ever was, the floor from the entry door and my bedroom door sloped down through the kitchen/dining area before leveling out just before the common wall with the other upstairs apartment. Depending upon their choice of chair, anyone sitting at the kitchen table faced uphill, leaned to the left, or leaned to the right. Cracked and peeling linoleum covered that floor, a sickly yellow with faded red, green, and blue streaks, making it look like someone vomited on it while passing through at speed, maybe on their way to the bathroom.

At the front of the house was the living room, the lone window was where I conducted my own "neighborhood watch" program. If nothing was happening, I could always pass the time picking at the always-peeling paint around the windows… probably no lead... probably... I'm fine. There was always something going on every Monday through Friday lunchtime, though, as a sulfur-blue cloud invaded the neighborhood after escaping from the blast furnace at Gould National Batteries two blocks down the street. It was a pretty cloud... probably not dangerous... probably... I'm fine.

Contributing to the creation of the cloud was the Max Phillips & Sons truck that made its way up and down McDonough Street once a week or so. Piled high with scrap metal for the factory, every time I saw it clank on by, I thought it would be the last. A Depression-Era relic, the truck was so old and dilapidated that I couldn't always tell where the heaping pile of junk ended and the truck began.

Like the kitchen floor, McDonough Street sloped, crossways. After some snow, passing vehicles would veer down to the curb and get stuck, Ma and I in the living room window counting casualties. Even a tow truck got stuck once, its back double wheels spinning, throwing snow on Old Lady Anthony's house, much to our delight. When the wheels spun through the snow, chunks of her husband's precious lawn pelted the house, providing one of the best laughs Ma and I ever shared.

For those times when the living room window lacked entertainment, we had a 13-inch black-and-white Motorola TV. The only station we could always get was WEAU Channel 13 in Eau Claire, an NBC affiliate. We had a radio I didn't much listen to except when Del was on it after he and Ma became an item. Then there was Ma's prized possession, a Magnavox console stereo. The only extravagance she had, it looked out of place, like the back porch storm windows and green drinking glass. But it sure sounded good, particularly when Ma played her Elvis, Herb Alpert,

Johnny Cash, Roy Orbison, Patsy Cline, and Dean Martin records.

As an only child, I had help keeping myself amused with a collection of Tonka, Matchbox, Hot Wheels, Tootsie Toy cars and trucks, and various games and blocks. Other than I couldn't shoot my Daisy Popgun in the house, Ma only had one rule regarding my toys - I had to put them away when I was done. Ma added another rule later after spending a curse-filled afternoon trying and failing to connect two pieces of track for a new toy.

"Here, Ma, let me do it," I then snapping the pieces together... in a snap.

"From now on, you put together your toys," and I did, although my vocabulary suffered.

I opened birthday and Christmas presents in that apartment. I watched game shows with Uncle Mike. I played cars and trucks with Uncle David. I built empires in the sandbox out back. Countless football and baseball games were played in the backyard with the neighbor kids. When it was bedtime, I'd wake Ma to tell her so, as she often fell asleep on the sofa, exhausted from working and going to school full-time.

One night, though, I woke her with more than a gentle nudge, sprinting across the living room and then leaping onto the sofa after coming face-to-face with the only monster I've ever seen. To this day, I can't explain what I saw standing in the corner of Ma's bedroom, but whatever it was, even if it was just my imagination, nothing ever terrified me more. To counter that encounter, it was in that apartment where I met Del, sitting at the kitchen table, facing uphill.

Ma and I slept on the south end, the high end, her bedroom in front with one west-facing window overlooking McDonough Street, mine in back with one south-facing window overlooking the Peterson's house on the corner, and the intersection of McDonough and East Madison Streets. When I couldn't or wouldn't sleep, I'd lie in bed watching the comings and goings. Because of the slope of the intersection, the headlights of vehicles heading east on Madison and then turning north onto McDonough would shine into my bedroom, creating a moving trail of shadows across the walls and ceiling.

Despite the light show that came in through my bedroom window, my favorite was the one I could see out of it - the flashing red light atop the telephone company's tower atop their downtown office building, over half a mile away. August 8, 1971, was the last night I saw that light from my bedroom. The next day, Ma and I moved to Waupaca. After we moved, I missed nothing more - Linus had his security blanket, and I had a blinking red light.

Such as it was, if the apartment had been nicer, the rent would've been more than Ma could afford, which wasn't much, which is why we were living there in the first place. Why the landlord was aware of Ma's financial situation - she a single mother raising a child while working full-time and studying full-time at the university. Why, in the eight years we lived there, Ray and Betty Wachs only raised the rent once, to $55.

Whenever I'm in Eau Claire, I try to make time for a drive-by because as old and decrepit as that apartment house was when I was a kid, it's still, still standing, almost my lifetime longer than I thought it would be. For all its shortcomings, 417½ McDonough Street really was only "half" a house, but it was a good home.

017

WINNER WINNER CHICKEN DINNER

The most memorable thing about Garfield's Restaurant was not the food but the "décor," an eye-stabbing mix of garish and cheap that screamed, "I dare you to eat here!" I'd never taken the dare, only passing by when I parked out back. I'd never set foot in Garfield's until Dan bought into it a few years after we graduated high school. Even then, I just hung out in the kitchen. While I lacked elbow room, my eyes were spared the visual assault of the neon lime green, hot pink, and orange-colored dining room.

The restaurant was located in the Waupaca Woods Mall. There used to be some woods, but the developer cut them down to build the mall. A supermarket and a discount department store anchored the ends, except they didn't open onto the actual mall sandwiched between. With an entry in the front and another in the back, siding the mall were no more than eight small businesses, including a hardware store, pharmacy, liquor store, and the restaurant.

As competition increased from growing shopping centers 30 minutes on either side of Waupaca, tenants came and went as the mall struggled to remain relevant. The supermarket and the pharmacy moved to new locations. The liquor store, notorious for its one-of-each inventory, eventually went out of business. So did the department and hardware stores. The one constant was the restaurant, located in the mall's back corner, even though, early on, business was anything but booming. I had the feeling that what few customers were ever there must've lacked the means, or the good sense, to dine elsewhere.

Garfield's was a fixer-upper if ever there was one. And that's just the kind of property that catches my eye, one with potential, especially in the right hands. Not only did I see what could be, but I also experienced what would be after Dan, the man with a plan to turn around Garfield's, bought out his partner. Garfield's would never be the same again. It would never be Garfield's again as Dan changed the name to Johnson's Waupaca Woods Restaurant.

Dan would leave his mark inside with his name now above the door. The food improved. So did the service. And mercifully, he changed the décor, then again, and again, and again.

"How many chicken dinners does a guy have to buy before you get it right?"

Over the years, the menu wasn't the only thing Dan expanded. After the liquor store held the shortest "Going Out of Business Sale" ever, Dan seized the opportunity to acquire the additional floor space, doubling the size of his restaurant.

A few years later, Dan expanded the restaurant again, pushing the mall's back wall into the parking lot to add more tables. Even with the twice-expanded dining room, customers still had to line up to get in on Friday nights and Saturday and Sunday mornings. Customers didn't seem to mind because Dan served good food in plentiful portions.

It's one reason why his is my favorite restaurant, and Sue's. So when I'm in Waupaca, The Woods is the restaurant I go to when the decision is mine. As I once told Dan, "Good thing I really like your restaurant because it wouldn't look good if others saw me dining at your competitors all the time." That's because Dan and I have been best friends since I moved to Waupaca the summer before we started third grade.

We hit it off almost immediately, our love of sports an early common denominator. At school, we lived for the playground. More than a few times during our two years at Westwood Elementary, we were the only ones who ventured outside during recess, in the dead of winter, in the cold, in the snow, when the playground sloped uphill, both ways. Because when the weather was particularly nasty, even for Wisconsin, teachers at Westwood permitted students to stay inside for recess.

Dan and I would have none of that. Recess? Inside? That was a slippery slope we weren't about to slide down. Show teachers you don't need recess, and next thing you know, you're in the sixth grade. Besides, we'd have the whole playground to ourselves for a rousing game of "snow-block football." We called it that because the football for our one-on-one games was a chunk of hard-packed snow carefully selected from the plowed piles bordering the school's parking lot. The best part was, out of sight, out of mind, our teacher, Mrs. Jome, sometimes forgot about us. So, while our classmates were sitting at their desks "learnin' junk," we were still outside, having so much fun that we never noticed hypothermia setting in.

While we were best friends, we looked an unlikely pair, as I was the tallest kid in class, and Dan, Dan was not. One day, while scouring the dictionary with classmates Marte and Bill because we didn't think our vocabulary was up to snuff, or hoping to learn some new dirty words - I forget which - we happened upon "tot *noun*: a small child."

Dan had a nickname. Before you pity him, Marte's nickname was Wiff, Bill's was BA, and mine was Snubber. Bill's was the only one that stuck through high school. Dan, along with Marte and I, would probably agree that was a good thing, and we can because all these years later, we're still friends.

Dan's favorite game to play was basketball. We played hundreds of one-on-one games over the years, whether on a school or city court, on the driveway at his parent's house, then later at his, or in the Waupaca Armory gym. In our younger days, we'd play to 100 points, two, three, even four times in an afternoon. We'd laugh about it years later, exhausted after playing to 20 once, maybe twice.

Early on, when I was a good head taller, the wins came easily for me, but even after Dan caught up and we were more or less the same size, I still found a way to win. In those hundreds of one-on-one games played over 20 years, Dan was always the loser. But I never saw him as one in anything that mattered, although just out of high school, someone did.

Sitting at the Oakwood Restaurant's bar one night, waiting for Dan to finish in the kitchen, a waitress asked, "Why do you hang out with that loser?" While she was talking about Dan, she wasn't referring to his many losses on the basketball court. "He'll be cooking chicken his whole life," she so thoughtfully added.

OK, as a cook at the Oakwood (Dan's last employer before buying into Garfield's), his nickname was The Chicken Man. What can I say? Even as a teenager, the guy knew his chicken and made mounds of it. Still, her words blindsided me. So, partly to recover from her attacking my friend and partly to make her uncomfortable for having done so, I waited an awkward amount of time before leaning in, focusing my gaze between her eyes, and then stating, with some authority, "Because I see something you don't... bitch."

As it turned out, she was right about one thing - Dan has been cooking chicken his whole life and many other delicious dishes as owner of his award-winning restaurant. He and his wife, the ever-bubbly Marsha, have built a highly successful business while raising Haley and Alexa, daughters any parents would be proud to call their own. Dan? Loser? I still chuckle when I think back to that night at the Oakwood.

Maybe she thought what she thought because Dan wasn't the best student in high school. While he had the smarts, high school offered little that interested him, the curriculum designed primarily for people like me, not Dan. Mr. Gohla's business class (Hello!) was the only one I ever recall him talking about, fondly. Even though he didn't excel in high school, I never doubted Dan would succeed, having witnessed his steely determination hundreds of times on the basketball court, even as his losses mounted.

Over the years, we'd never spoken of the long winning streak, or losing streak, depending upon your perspective. We just played as the friends we'd been since he was eight and I was nine years old. When I was a head taller, Dan could've blamed his losses on our size difference, but he never did. Years later, when we were more evenly matched, I know losing frustrated him, even though he did his best never to let it show.

But one summer day, well beyond our high school years, below Waupaca's water tower on a court just off Hillcrest Drive, the winning basket was Dan's. Not that I let it show, but I was happy for him because, as you've probably figured out, the only reason I had the opportunity to beat him so many times over so many years was because Dan never quit. Winners never do.

018

WE'RE CHICKENS

"He controls the corn in this territory."

"You sure? We're about to go inside his house."

"Oh, you're the new girl. Yeah, yeah, he's the one. Been the main supplier for years."

"Where does he keep his corn?"

"In that bucket over there."

"But that bucket has a lid. How can he get inside?"

"Opposable thumbs."

"Opposable thumbs?"

"Yeah, if we had some, we could help ourselves."

"I wish I had opposable thumbs. Those humans, they can do anything."

"What do you mean?"

"Well, look at the way that human can change his color. I'm mostly white. You're mostly black. But that human? One day, he'll be red on top and blue on the bottom. The next day, he's yellow on top and green on the bottom. How does he do that?"

"I get it. Like the day he was colored Zubaz."

"Zubaz?"

"Yeah, looked like somebody barfed on him in red and white."

"I'd like to see that. Is he colored Zubaz often?"

"No, no, he's married now."

"For a guy who controls the corn, he has just the one bucket?"

"Rumor has it he's got many more in his bodega."

"Bodega? What's a bodega?"

"I don't know. It's a Spanish thing. I think you're supposed to poop in it."

"Does he make us earn the corn?"

"Nah. He just gives it away."

"Really?"

"Yeah, he's some wacky shutterbug. Likes to take photos of us. Shows them to his family and friends."

"Humans like looking at pictures of chickens?"

"I guess so. Apparently, they think we're funny."

"Funny ha-ha or funny strange?"

"Little of each. You know Henrietta, right?"

"Hey, what's this?"

"It's called a welcome mat."

"I don't understand"

"It means we're welcome to poop on it."

"Still, kind of risky going inside his house, isn't it?"

"Maybe, but we've been making a lot of noise out here on his back porch, and he hasn't noticed."

"So we just walk right in?"

"Desperate times call for desperate measures. Sometimes you gotta work to get his attention."

"But what about that dog of his, Packers? He's pretty big. I've watched him chase down sticks and balls. He's scary good at it."

"Nah, he's OK. One day, we dared Henrietta to run past him. Nothing."

"Yeah, Henrietta will do anything. Maybe that's why she lays so many eggs."

"No worries, these two will keep an eye on him. Let's go in."

"Wow! Nice coop!"

"Oh, rooster, that's a pretty big selection of pots he's got in the kitchen. I've heard stories."

"Relax, nobody ever goes missing from this yard. Now at the neighbor's... different story."

"Hey, what's that?"

"Humans call it a throw rug."

"What's it for?"

"No one knows. My guess? You're supposed to poop on it. C'mon, focus. We're here for corn."

"But he's just sitting there. What's he doing?"

"Watching TV."

"TV? What's TV?"

"It's hard to explain, but humans like watching other humans in make-believe comedic situations."

"Why not go out and watch them for real?"

"Because watching humans on TV, he can laugh and curse at them without having to worry about being polite."

"Polite? What's polite?"

"Not sure. I think it has something to do with not pooping where you're not supposed to."

"Hey, where's everybody else?"

"Outside, still on the porch. Can't be too careful. If this mission goes sideways, at least a few will survive to warn the others."

"Smart."

"Hey, we're chickens."

"So what happens now?"

"Well, usually we have to wait for a commercial, then he'll get up. If not, we poop on his floor."

"Pooping on the floor gets us corn?"

"Always. He doesn't like anyone pooping on his ceramic tile. You should've seen what he did to the dog after he pooped on it."

"Bad, huh?"

"Well, you see all the pipe Packers lays out in the yard? He isn't doing that in the house anymore."

"Look! Look! An ad for erectile dysfunction! He's getting up! He's up!"

"Scramble! Scramble! Corn! Corn! Glorious corn!"

019

YOU'RE A FATHER!

"Male or female?"

"I'm not sure."

"Ummm, Riyad, do I need to have a talk with you about the birds and the bees?"

"Ha! No, no, I'm not sure because I've never really seen it."

"Ummm, Riyad, are you sure you even have a kitten?"

"Yes, yes, but it hides in the bathroom."

"OK, if it's a female, I'll take it, but if it's a male, then no. I don't want a tomcat peeing on my new carpet and howlin' to go prowlin' all hours of the night."

"OK. I'll see if I can find out."

Riyad and I worked in the same department on the Men's Campus of United Arab Emirates University. We were also neighbors in the Al Khabisi sector of Al Ain, our villas less than a block apart. After Riyad and his wife, Bernadette, returned to theirs after the summer holiday, they discovered that while they were away, the maid let their housecat go outside… and the cat came back the very next day, pregnant. Since Bernadette came back from her summer holiday, also pregnant, she and Riyad had concerns about toxoplasmosis, so either the cat with kittens or the pregnant wife had to go.

"1 cute Kitten seeks a home," read the purple magic-markered words on the sheet of A4 paper folded and thumbtacked to the bulletin board outside our office. I can only imagine the response if the sign had said, "1 cute Wife seeks a home," had the decision gone the other way. Before Riyad posted the ad, a friend had taken care of most of their problem, agreeing to take their cat and two of the three kittens. For reasons unknown, they did not take the third.

I never really had a pet of my own, but now, with my first "real" job and a home I could finally call my own, sort of, I decided getting a cute kitten might be a good idea. It would add some life to my cavernous villa because except for a TV, mini-stereo, computer, refrigerator, two-burner hotplate, washing machine, mattress, carpeting, drapes, and a couple of two-ton (24,000BTU) through-the-wall air conditioners (it got scorching hot in Al Ain), it was essentially empty. And with no Internet back then and nothing much on TV when there was TV, a kitty could keep me company.

So I was delighted when Riyad popped by my office a couple of days later and proclaimed, "John! Congratulations! You're a father!"

"OK, great! When would be a good time to pick up cute kitten?"

"How about after work?

"Sounds good!"

Before I was to pick up cute kitten, the last bit of work for the day was a teacher training session, one especially for new faculty, as I was. The session's title? "How To Count To Ten." They don't hire just anyone to teach at the university level. I should mention the lesson on how to count to ten would be presented in

German by a native speaker, a young man named Jonathan. Because I'd seen so many reruns of the TV show *Hogan's Heroes*, I figured I had a good head start after hearing Sergeant Schultz count the POWs at roll call, "Eins, zwei, drei..." more times than I could count.

The exercise aimed to underscore how difficult even the simplest lesson could be when presented in a foreign language. We might then appreciate how our students would feel listening to us natter on since many of them didn't understand English all that well, if at all.

A second, unexpected lesson on how to count to ten, presented in Arabic by a native speaker, a distinguished gent named Kamil, further hammered home the point. I never felt so stupid... "Wahid, ithnaan, thalaatha... You're just making these words up, aren't you, Kamil?"

One number caught our attention, the Arabic word for "9" - "tissa'a" - spelled correctly, phonetically anyway. Why isn't phonetically spelled phonetically? If you're wondering, the apostrophe in tissa'a is one of those glottal stop things, so just choke a bit when pronouncing the a'a.

Tissa'a. Catchy it was. We were saying it repeatedly, like Timmy says, "Timmy!" on the *South Park* TV show. I'm sure the site of Westerners repeatedly saying 9 in Arabic, for no particular reason to no one in particular, puzzled the locals on the UAE University Men's Campus as we made our way to the parking lot at the end of the session and our workday. "Tissa'a! Tissa'a! Tissa'a!" As I said, they don't hire just anyone to teach at the university level.

With the word still bouncing around in my head and my new Honda Civic still on a ship somewhere between Japan and the UAE, Riyad gave me a lift to his home to pick up cute kitten. With every 9 I saw, whether on a license plate, road sign, billboard, or whatever, I was saying tissa'a in my head. Maybe out loud. Probably in my head. Maybe out loud.

On the way, Riyad further explained cute kitten's history. Separated from her mother too soon, friends had already housed her in three homes before he and his wife returned and made it four. Having had her for only a week, Riyad said she spent most of her time hiding in the ceramic pedestal of a bathroom sink.

Once at the sink, I discovered there was a hole in the back of the pedestal providing access to the drainpipe. About a foot-and-a-half off the floor and with the pedestal's slick surface, I didn't see how a kitten could get in the hole, but the hisses and spits emanating from within told me I was wrong. Reaching blindly into the hole, I had no idea what I was going after other than it was a kitten. Like my yet-to-be-delivered Honda, acquiring things sight unseen had become a trend since my arrival in Al Ain.

The only way it would've been easier to reach around, in, and down that hole would have been with a dislocated shoulder. As it was, I nearly lost a hand before I finally got hold of the surprisingly strong kitten, one that put up quite a fight to avoid being evicted from her home before I somehow managed to yank her up and out of the pedestal. It wasn't a pleasant experience for either of us, my hand covered in blood, she in cute kitten pee.

Twisting and turning to get away like no cat I'd ever seen, much less a kitten, I got her into a Riyad-supplied cardboard box that previously held a dozen 1.5-liter bottles of Al Ain Water, bottles that didn't bite and scratch. Riyad and I quickly closed the top of the box as cute kitten was still doing the (Warner Brothers cartoon version) Tasmanian devil thing inside. Just wild she was.

"John, you sure about this?"

"No problem. I'm good with animals. She'll be OK."

"You have a name for her?"

Even though I hadn't thought about it, I didn't need to, "Tissa'a."

So, down the block I walked with a Tissa'a-filled cardboard box. I still hadn't gotten a good look at her when I opened the box at the door of an empty bedroom in my villa, Tissa'a immediately sprinting across the room and head first into the patio doors, hitting them so hard I was surprised, but relieved she didn't break the glass or her neck.

It didn't occur to me until later that letting her loose in a large open space when she'd spent most of her life in a confined one was perhaps not the smartest thing I could've done. She kept head-butting the glass, to no avail, before I scrambled to collect her, returning Tissa'a to the cardboard box before she hurt herself or the door.

"Tissa'a, you're gonna have to learn what glass is."

I put the box in the powder room and closed the door, the wooden door. The room was small enough that she couldn't get a running start into any doors or walls, I not wanting any broken necks. The only window was well out of reach and featured a ventilation fan so she'd get plenty of fresh air. And like the kitchen and the other bathrooms in my villa, the walls and floor were tiled, and there was a floor drain for easy cleaning.

Setting the box on its side in a corner next to the toilet, I opened the flaps slowly, half expecting Tissa'a to leap out and wrap herself around my head, biting and scratching until I stopped making noise. Instead, realizing there was no escape, she remained in the far corner, hissing and spitting at me.

In the short time she'd been my kitten, I'd already thought of several adjectives to describe her, cute not among them. She was the first kitten I ever saw that wasn't, especially since she was filthy… and smelly. Kittens were supposed to be little fur balls. Tissa'a was something else. Built like a bulldog, even as a kitten, she was a solid mass of muscle with claws thick like a dog's but pointy like a cat's, a dangerous combination, as I discovered reaching inside the sink pedestal.

I sat on the powder room floor nearly every opportunity over the next couple-two-three weeks, there not any furniture to sit on in the rest of the villa anyway. Besides, Tissa'a needed a friend, and so did I, why I got her in the first place, so my home wouldn't feel so empty. Playing solitaire to help pass the time, I'd talk to Tissa'a as she crouched in the far corner of her box, waiting to pounce if I moved in her direction. When I'd reach over to place playing cards on the foundation piles, she'd hiss and spit, letting me know my hand was getting too close for her comfort.

Unfortunately, her disposition didn't change over those couple-two-three weeks. She just stayed in that box, hissing and spitting at me. The only evidence she ever left, left in the litter box on the other side of the toilet. Discouraged, the day came when I wondered if Tissa'a was beyond my help. While I thought it, I wouldn't accept it, I couldn't accept it. I refused to give up on her.

Instead, I decided to shake things up by not closing the door to the powder room that night so I could hear Tissa'a if she did something other than hiss and spit. I blocked the powder room door using the empty cardboard box that once contained my new refrigerator.

Just the right width to fit inside the door's frame, there was still plenty of space above the box for sound to escape.

It did the trick because later that night, I awoke to an insistent banging from the powder room. As I peered around the hallway corner, I discovered the noise was Tissa'a, head-butting the refrigerator box as she'd done to the patio doors when I first let her loose in my villa. A few head-butts later, she'd pushed the huge refrigerator box just far enough to squeeze her way out the bathroom door.

Darting across the hall and into the kitchen, she wedged herself behind the refrigerator the box had come in. When I peeked behind the fridge, there was Tissa'a, looking terribly uncomfortable in a position that appeared even more awkward than mine when I retrieved her from inside the sink pedestal. As I leaned in for a better look, she didn't hiss and spit, instead giving me a meow. With a smile, I turned and headed back to bed, knowing something special was behind my fridge… a desert cat named Tissa'a.

020

SNOWBALL FIGHT

"WHAT THE HELL IS GOING ON HERE?"
"…..snowball fight…"
"GET THIS SNOW OUT OF HERE! NOW!" demanded Ricky, the Resident Assistant on 4th Floor North of the Hugunin Hall dormitory, before slip-sliding into his room and slamming the door behind him. As the slam reverberated off the hallway walls, we looked around and saw what Ricky saw - snow splattered on the doors, walls, even the ceiling, and the rust-colored carpet in the hallway, just installed over the winter break, buried in snow, a foot deep in places.

As Resident Assistant, Ricky was the responsible adult and the stand-in parent for the other 32 students on the wing. For me, he was a bit too much of a stand-in, Ricky a neighbor of my Uncle Rick and Aunt Beth when he returned home to Jim Falls, a small town in northwest Wisconsin. Ricky's was a thankless job, although he got a room to himself and a small stipend. Some RA's took their job seriously, others, not so much, but that night, Ricky was deadly serious, the look on his face a combination of shock and awe.

Hugunin Hall was a typical university dorm. Not only did it look like almost every other dorm on the

University of Wisconsin-Platteville campus, but it looked like almost every other dorm on every other UW campus. Four floors high because five would've required the installation of elevators, it had that drab institutional look with its tan brick façade and single-pane aluminum-framed windows. Concrete block walls divided each of Hugunin's two wings into 17 dorm rooms lining the perimeter.

Inside the squared O-shaped plan was the bathroom with four sinks, four stalls, one urinal, four showers, and the janitor's closet that also provided access to the trash chute. At one corner of the wing was a door to a stairwell that opened directly to the outside on the ground floor. On the opposite corner, there was a door to the other wing. Sandwiched between wings was a seldom-used lounge with an old TV and uncomfortable sofas and chairs with rounded corners and edges so students wouldn't hurt themselves.

For each resident, each double-occupancy room had a single bed that doubled as a sofa during the day, a small closet, a dresser, a desk, a bookshelf, a chair, and a round metal wastebasket. Below the one window was a hot water radiator, how far the window left open, the thermostat. Living in the dorm was good training for anyone with a career in crime ahead, the Spartan rooms comparable to prison cells.

Maybe Hugunin Hall's prison vibe contributed to the hostility triggering the snowball fight in the room next door. Perhaps it was the pressure of school or paying for it. Maybe it was the freedom of being away from home without parental supervision. Or it could've been too much alcohol consumption.

Whatever the reason, personalities sometimes clashed…

<SPLAT>

Andy never saw it coming. Watching TV in his dorm room with the radiator cranking out the heat on a cold winter night, I'm sure the last thing he expected was anyone pelting him with a snowball. But on the way back from the cafeteria after dinner, his roommate, Dave, scooped up some snow, compacted it to size, and carried it up to their room, "Pearl Harboring" Andy square in the chest.

"YOU BASTARD! I WILL KILL YOU!"

The only indoor snowball fight I'd ever see soon spread to neighboring rooms, then down and around the hall. Few knew who threw the first snowball or why, but it wasn't long before the whole wing was involved for no other reason than everyone else was doing it, much to the chagrin of mothers everywhere. Alliances formed between roommates, even Dave and Andy, no one wanting to make an enemy of the relative stranger with 24-hour access to their stuff.

As is the case in many a battle, some locations had strategic advantages over others. Rooms on corners had a line of sight down two hallways to two other corners. Those with rooms near the bathroom could add tap water to their snowballs, making them iceballs. Residents in rooms near the stairwell had easier access to the endless supply of snow outside.

Soon realizing winter coat pockets couldn't hold enough snowballs to make climbing eight flights of stairs worthwhile, emptied dorm-issued wastebaskets were carried outside, filled with snow, and brought up to the fourth floor of Hugunin Hall again and again and again. Lasting a couple-two-three hours, the snowball fight turned our once toasty wing into a winter wonderland, especially after we opened all the windows to help keep the snow from melting so it could be recycled.

We were having a blast, the wing reveling in the opportunity to blow off more than a little steam until Ricky returned and blew off some of his own. The snowball fight over, we agreed that roommates were responsible for removing the snow in the hallway outside their door. Cleanup still took an hour or so, even though we didn't have to haul all that snow downstairs. Instead, we disposed of it out of our already open windows.

Early the following morning, though, Ricky was up and still angry. "LOOK AT THIS CARPET! HOUSING IS GOING TO KILL YOU GUYS!" Another door slamming followed. University housing would make us pay for any damage done beyond normal wear and tear, especially since the carpet was new. Once again, we saw what Ricky saw - melting snow had stained the almost new carpet from wall to wall, hall to hall. It looked terrible, but at least that new carpet smell was finally gone.

Even so, all was ignored until May, the snow outside long gone, when Ricky again reminded us of the price we'd pay if housing had to take care of the carpet problem we'd not. So, with the end of the semester drawing near, we rented a Rug Doctor from a downtown store in hopes of cleaning the carpet. We nominated the guy with the pickup truck to pick up the carpet-cleaning machine, and the rest of us chipped in to cover the rental cost. Getting the bulky Rug Doctor up to the fourth floor was a chore, but most everyone helped with that, too.

Like the snow removal the night of the snowball fight, we agreed that roommates were responsible for cleaning the carpet outside their dorm room door. But after witnessing the machine's magic, it wasn't long before everyone was clamoring for a turn at the controls because that Rug Doctor... really sucked. Not only did we return our hallway carpet to like-new in no time, but we also moved the furniture out of our rooms so we could clean even more carpet. With many residents, including me, set to return to the same wing the following school year, we saw an opportunity to do what university housing hadn't done in years - clean the decrepit carpet in our rooms.

Ricky seemed quite pleased after taking a lap around the wing to ensure all was in order. Not only would university housing have billed us if it were not, but the stained carpet would've reflected badly on Ricky as a Resident Assistant. Ricky was a good guy and a good RA. We didn't want to make (more) trouble for him.

"Looks good, guys. Real good. Could I use the Rug Doctor to clean my room?"

"No worries, Ricky! We'll do it for you!

021

THE BUICK'S LAST RIDE

"Wanna get some ice cream?"

Seems an innocent start to a story, but within minutes, the story would come within inches of leading off the 10 o'clock local TV news. Even though another roll of the wheels was all that separated us from a disaster of headline proportions, before the night was over Del would still need a new car, the story of what happened, what really happened, a secret Jay and I kept for years.

It was the summer of '72, the first Ma and I spent in Eau Claire after moving to Waupaca in August of '71. We were a two-household family, with Del working at Eau Claire's WOKL 1050 Radio and his son Jay attending North High School. That summer, though, after Ma and I were both out of school - she a teacher at Waupaca High, me a student at Westwood Elementary - we closed up the house in Waupaca and moved to Eau Claire, just for the summer, Ma and Del renting a house on Erin Street on the city's north side.

Just a block from where I was born, it was only a few blocks from Del's parents, Elmer and Erna, on Putnam Street, where Del and Jay lived the rest of the year. Only a few blocks beyond was our old apartment on McDonough Street, and a few blocks more, one of my favorite places, Gustafson's Ice Cream Store.

The décor was Edward Hopper's *Nighthawks* diner stark, but almost everything we ever bought was for takeaway anyway. Countless times, Del, Ma, and I (Jay, a teenager, often had better things to do) would pile into Del's metallic green Buick station wagon and go to Gustafson's, where each of us ordered a cone. Del also asked for a cup of ice water for afterward.

The only flavor of ice cream ever in our fridge was vanilla or its cultured cousin, French vanilla. At Gustafson's, though, there were more choices than any grocery store's frozen food section. So many that even though I always got what I wanted, I always felt I missed something, especially if I was permitted a two-scoop cone when deciding what flavor combination to order took longer than the eating. But then, imagining all the possibilities was half the fun. So, not quite ten when just-turned-seventeen Jay asked, "Wanna get some ice cream?" I was out the door before he was.

Gustafson's was 14 blocks away, located off Birch Street at the foot of Eau Claire's highest point, Mt. Tom. Ice cream run or not, I was always up for a ride in Del's Buick. I loved that car, the third of the station wagon's three-row bench seating faced backward, out the tailgate window, encouraging me to make faces at drivers behind the Buick's back bumper. Sure, that could be entertaining, but what I enjoyed most was the alternate perspective resulting from going forward while facing backward, especially at speed.

Ma and Del were out that night, probably at the Ramada Inn off the interstate, attending a seminar on "How To Make Your Children's Demise Look Like an Accident." Since Del always drove, why they took Ma's car instead of his, I don't know. The first car Ma ever owned, she nicknamed the sky blue Plymouth Fury III Mehitabel, from Don Marquis' 1927 book *archy and mehitabel*, a collection of poems and short stories featuring two fictional characters, a cockroach named Archy and his best friend, a streetwise alley cat in her ninth life, including one as Cleopatra, named Mehitabel.

A philosophical cockroach, Archy, a free verse poet in an earlier life, wrote stories and poems on an old typewriter in the newspaper office after everyone had gone home for the day. In the book, Archy's words were in lowercase letters because he typed by jumping from key to key and couldn't simultaneously press shift and a letter. Archy's accounts of his daily adventures with Mehitabel, featured in New York's Evening Sun newspaper, were satiric commentary on daily living on the city's rowdy streets. With that backstory, perhaps Del didn't want Jay, who'd just gotten his driver's license, to drive Ma's car in case he should go for a spin.

Until Jay turned right off Birch Street, two blocks before Gustafson's, I had no idea he had more on his mind than ice cream. Whether his side trip was a spur-of-the-moment decision or something he cooked up before we left the house, I don't know, but either way, we were on our way to a place I'd never been - the top of Mt. Tom. Despite growing up in the neighborhood and roving far on my bike, I'd never been to the top of Mt. Tom. That night would be my first and last time.

Connecting the top and bottom of Mt. Tom was a one-lane asphalt road. If the city was serious about preventing joyriders from driving to the top, they should've put up more than just a sign saying "ROAD CLOSED." Sure, we would've moved any barricade out of the way or thrown it in the back of the Buick, but at least we would've had to work to access the top of Mt.

Tom. While Jay paid the sign no-never-mind, he switched off the car's headlights to not give us away to any neighborhood snitches or Eau Claire's cops.

After the paved portion of the road ended at the leveled-off top, Jay continued slow-rolling until he figured he'd gone as far as he could. "Figured" because we couldn't see the edge of the drop-off. We found it, though, after getting out and walking toward the front of the car, not quite making it before we stepped over the edge in tandem, falling back on our backsides lest we go tumbling down the hill. Jay had stopped the car just in time, the bumper over the edge, the front wheels inches from it, how close we came to careening down the north side of Mt. Tom in Del's Buick.

"Good thing I set the parking brake."

"Yeah, smart."

Even though we were at the top of Eau Claire, we were disappointed that there wasn't much to see other than the city lights twinkling through the many trees. If not for the thrill of nearly rolling over the edge, our excursion to the top would've been underwhelming. Nevertheless, we were sufficiently satisfied, having thumbed our noses at the "ROAD CLOSED" sign to conquer Mt. Tom in the dark.

Mission accomplished, we hopped back into the Buick. Minutes later, Jay parked the car in front of Gustafson's Ice Cream Store, located in a small commercial center that included, among other enterprises, a laundromat, gas station, VFW hall, and Shorty's Barber Shop. Only after Jay and I opened the car doors did we notice the smoke billowing from beneath the Buick.

"Sonofabitch!"

Jay had forgotten to release the parking brake, burning out the transmission of his father's station wagon on the drive down Mt. Tom. His telephone call to his father was difficult, even though his story never mentioned the side trip, much less his nearly driving over the edge at the top of Mt. Tom. Instead, his story, our story, was one of two innocent boys making an innocent trip to Gustafson's for ice cream.

Our story had a couple of holes, however... "Why was the parking brake set?" A fair question, given that it rarely was on a car with an automatic transmission. Then came another fair question... "You didn't notice the parking brake was set, for a mile?" Our shrugs and befuddled looks explained what we could not and would not.

If Jay had told the truth, I suppose he could've claimed that had he not set the parking brake, the Buick may have rolled down Mt. Tom and crashed into a house - assuming it would've crossed the always-busy Birch Street without incident - in hopes that apocalyptic scenario would cause Del and Ma to forget about the smoldering transmission.

Our trip to the top of Mt. Tom and then to Gustafson's for ice cream we didn't get would be the Buick's last ride, Del not paying for a new transmission, the old car not worth the expense. Instead, the Buick's next stop was the junkyard. Del then bought a new Dodge Polara to replace his station wagon.

Years later, Jay finally fessed up, telling Del the whole truth about how the parking brake that burned out the transmission on his Buick came to be set. Until then, I'd never said a word because before Jay called Del from Gustafson's, he warned me, "Don't you dare tell Pa or your mother the truth."

Not the first time Jay told me that. Nor the last.

022

I'LL NEVER FORGET MY FIRST

"Park here," said my driver's test examiner as he motioned toward the curb on Washington Street. So I signaled, did the mirror, mirror, blindspot thing, and eased over to the curb on the quiet street with no other parked cars. On an uphill grade, once parked, I turned the wheels to the left, as my instructor, Mr. Colbert, taught me to do in my Driver's Education class at Waupaca High School. It was a safety thing, so if the car somehow started rolling downhill on its own, with the wheels turned to the left, the curb would prevent it from moving any further.

"You should turn your wheels to the right when parking uphill, not left."

"I was taught the opposite in Driver's Ed."

"If you do that, your car could roll up and over the curb, then back down and into oncoming traffic."

"Has that ever happened?"

"Yes."

"So it's better to have a car roll onto a sidewalk than into traffic?" The grim look on his face told me he believed it was.

To demonstrate his point, he instructed me to "Shift into neutral, then take your foot off the brake."

As expected, the car rolled backward, stopping when the right front tire hit the curb. "Isn't that what's supposed to happen?"

"Yes, yes, but if the car has enough momentum, it can continue rolling." He then opened the door, unbuckling his seatbelt to get a better look at the right front wheel. Propping himself between his seat and the open car door, he instructed me to "Shift into reverse, then give it some gas."

If I did what he asked, I'd end up backing downhill into traffic. While it would prove his point, I didn't see how a parked car could build up enough momentum to go up and over a curb after rolling just a few inches, except maybe on the steep Garfield Avenue hill in Eau Claire, where not coincidentally, there was no parking. Nevertheless, I didn't want to antagonize the man standing in the way of obtaining my first driver's license, so I shifted the car into reverse.

"Hit the gas."

"But…" concerned my examiner's position looked a precarious one, he half in and half out of the car.

"Hit it."

The car jumped the curb and then continued rolling. Up to that point, my driver's test had gone well, but when the right front wheel dropped back into the gutter and the car door flung wide open, my examiner lost his balance… and his grip.

"This can't be happening," I muttered to myself, gazing upon the fedora-wearing old man, arms and legs pointing in every direction, struggling to recombobulate himself, he in the gutter, his clipboard planted in the snowbank on the side of the street. I leaned over, extending a hand to help him back into the car.

"Are you OK?"

"Yes… I think so."

As one of the oldest students in my class, I was one of the first to have an opportunity to get my hands on the Holy Grail for 16-year-olds - a valid driver's license. Having already failed my first attempt, a second failure now seemed certain. I mean, who has a driver's test examiner fall out of their car and into a gutter during an exam and still passes?

Having proved his point, I guess, the exam continued for five of the most awkward minutes I've ever experienced. Even though I figured the rest was pointless, I did my best, finishing with a perfect parallel park. He said nothing as I followed him from the car to the Department of Motor Vehicles office. While he completed his paperwork, I had a few excruciating minutes to ponder how to explain another driving test fail to Ma and Del, my friends, and my Driver's Ed. instructor, Mr. Colbert.

Mr. Colbert was the former head basketball coach at Waupaca High. A great coach who got the most out of his players, he was as intense in his classroom as on the basketball court. In a different time, when teachers could discipline students, he once used his large frame to hold a school bully up against some lockers as he explained "the situation" while using the student's nose to juice an orange half someone discarded in the hallway.

My first time driving with Mr. Colbert, I was shocked after he told me to head to the highway. Sensing my apprehension, as not only was snow falling, it was blowing and drifting, he, without an orange half, explained the situation, "J (he always called me "J"), you live in Wisconsin. You have to learn to drive in the snow. Today, we have snow. So learn."

Mr. Colbert liked me. I liked Mr. Colbert. While we had a good time tooling around town, he always explaining, taking advantage of teachable moments whenever they arose. One time, while driving down Main Street, I'd not spotted a car backing out of an angled parking space. Pumping the instructor's brakes, he brought the car to a safe stop.

"J, you're younger and have faster reflexes, but I have experience. Always scan the road ahead for potential problems so you won't need those reflexes."

"Yes, sir!"

When I'd completed the required hours behind the wheel, Mr. Colbert told me, "J, you're ready to take the driving test. You'll have no problem passing." Knowing he wouldn't say it if he didn't mean it, I made an appointment to take my first driving exam. Waupaca's DMV office was open only two days per week as the staff rotated amongst other small towns in the area.

Waiting my turn, the younger of the two examiners called my name. We walked across the street to Ma's car, angle-parked in a municipal lot. Little did I know that before I'd finished backing out of that parking space, I'd already failed, even though the exam went well, so I thought, with only one maneuver remaining.

"Parallel park here," he commanded, motioning to a parking space, again on Washington Street, this time adjacent to the municipal lot where the exam began. My spatial aptitude told me there was no way I could parallel park in the space - it too small for the car. At that moment, I realized the examiner wanted me to fail, but I didn't know why.

"It's impossible," I said. "That space is too small for this car."

"Parallel park."

So I gave it a go. What choice did I have? Even though that parallel park was one of my best ever, I couldn't overcome the geometry of the situation. While

I managed to get the car as far into the space as possible, it was not all the way in - failure to execute a parallel park reason enough for my examiner to fail me.

"You're way too far from the curb."

"I told you. This space isn't big enough."

"Yes, it is. Come on, I'll show you." So we stepped out into the street. Checking the gaps between the cars, we saw there was not enough room to stand at either end of Ma's midsized sedan. I think even the examiner was surprised at how small the space was and how close I came to foiling his plot anyway.

"It's simple: the diagonal length of this car is longer than the length of this parking space." While the examiner intended to show me it was possible, his expression told me he didn't appreciate my impromptu geometry lesson explaining why it was not.

"You couldn't parallel park this car in this space. No one could because there isn't enough room."

"Yes, there is."

"No, there's not, asshole."

Oops…

OK, I knew I'd failed, but I also knew that remark could have ramifications, I already thinking, "Maybe I could take the next exam in Eau Claire."

Once we returned to the municipal lot, my examiner informed me, "You failed."

"Really, Captain Obvious?" I thought to myself, one remark too late.

"You were too confident when you backed out of the parking space at the start of the exam. I decided to fail you then."

"Did I do anything wrong?"

"No, you were just overconfident."

Shaking my head in disgust, I almost called him an asshole again.

Sue will tell you I can drive backward with the best of them. A former colleague, Ed, would tell you the same after I once drove him across the UAE University Women's Campus, straight as an arrow, backward, at 50 mph. Ed was both mortified and impressed, but driving backward has never been a problem for me. Perhaps one reason why piloting the Chief Waupaca came so easy as it steered from the back when going forward, the same as a car when driving backward.

Of course, everyone wanted to know why I failed my driving test, one Mr. Colbert expected me to pass easily. I told the truth about the parallel park, but not the whole truth, worried what I'd said would get back to Ma, and I wouldn't get my driver's license until I was 28, when she got hers.

After failing, I had to wait a few weeks before I could make an appointment for a second driving test. I never imagined the examiner for that one would "end up" in the gutter on Washington Street. So when he told me, "Congratulations, you passed," I was stunned. With an appreciative handshake and a "Thank you, sir," I may have been the only 16-year-old who passed their driver's test but looked like they'd failed.

Exiting the DMV, driver's license in hand, I was dumbfounded… "Of the two tests I took, the one where my examiner fell out of the car and into the gutter… was the one I passed?" There was a time, some 30 years later, when I would simultaneously hold valid driver's licenses from three countries on three continents, but I'll never forget my first.

023

QUEPASACONSUBASURA

"Say what?" Sue and I had hardly gotten settled in our new home off a dead-end dirt (we did not yet aspire to gravel) road on the side of a mountain in a remote area of southern Ecuador. Nevertheless, every Friday evening with clockwork regularity, one of our neighbors would inquire, "¿Quepasaconsubasura?"

While I studied Spanish for four years at Waupaca High School, I soon realized that after more than 25 years, not only had my hearing gotten worse, but so too had my Spanish. And Sue? Growing up in Calgary, French, the only other language she exposed to in school, Quepasaconsubasura was not in her limited Spanish vocabulary. Cerveza and no were, but Sue's never used those words in the same sentence. Ever.

We were used to hearing foreign languages as we'd just moved from the United Arab Emirates, where a large and diverse expat population made the country a language cornucopia. For starters, we regularly heard Arabic, Hindi, Urdu, and Farsi, along with the UAE's least common denominator language, broken English. In the Emirates, we'd heard almost every language there was to hear, except the one we needed to know after moving to Ecuador - Spanish.

After a few weeks, we jokingly wondered if our new Ecuadorian neighbors were drawing straws to determine who'd get the "privilege" of making the weekly inquiry, "¿Quepasaconsubasura?" It didn't matter who asked, the result was always the same. I'd end up feeling stupid, wondering what good my years of university education and four years of high school Spanish were when the neighbor's thigh-high children understood the question I could not, "¿Quepasaconsubasura?"

No matter how often I asked our neighbors to repeat their question, or repeat it more slowly, it didn't matter. Moreover, not knowing what they were saying, their question sounded like one long, long-winded word, "¿Quepasaconsubasura?"

Google Translate? English/Spanish translation books? We had access to each, but because we couldn't understand the question, we didn't know what to look up, like trying to find the spelling of a word in a dictionary - if I knew how to spell the word, I could find it, but then I wouldn't need to look it up. Because for all the Spanish I still remembered, my hearing wouldn't allow me to make out the one word in the question critical to a successful translation - basura.

Players in a twisted game of *Jeopardy*, we had the answer but didn't understand the question until we happened upon the keyword in the Vilcabamba town square. There it was, in white-stenciled letters on a park-green-painted trashcan, the word "BASURA."

"TRASH! Our neighbors want to know what we're doing with our trash!"

There was much rejoicing.

Experts say when you learn a foreign language, a good way to begin is to find a word you can own - a word you can pronounce and use confidently because you know it well. In addition to cerveza and no, basura became such a word for Sue. While she may one day forget the Spanish she's since learned, my guess is she'll never forget the Spanish word for trash. Neither will I.

Now prepared with our newly owned word, we couldn't wait for Friday evening. After the neighbor drawing the short straw approached our gate and engaged us in conversation, eventually came the question we were waiting for, "¿Qué pasa con su basura?" With a knowing grin, I repeated the question and told our neighbor, in my best Spanish, that we were taking our trash to the municipal bins in town. The smile on his face told me all I needed to know - he understood my reply.

So, with a good laugh and the usual handshakes all around, our Friday evening conversations with the neighbors over our trash situation ended. A couple of years later, the municipality started a trash collection service on our dead-end dirt (we aspired to gravel) road. Every other Monday, and now every Wednesday, barrio residents put out their trash bags, and no one needs to ask, "¿Qué pasa con su basura?"

024

NUMBERS FIRST

"Hot." My first word. I don't remember saying it or learning it, but my Grandma Curran taught it to me to explain why I shouldn't touch the rust-colored behemoth of a space heater in the living room of our apartment on McDonough Street. Like me, you might not remember learning your first word, but if you've ever learned another language, you might remember your first foreign word.

Mainly because "they" say that when learning a foreign language, you should start by finding a word you can own. It builds the confidence you'll need when conjugating irregular verbs in something other than the present tense. I never understood grammar in my first language to a level I could explain to myself or others, but give me a test, and I'd test out of English, as I did at three universities without taking an English class.

However, I would not test out of Spanish, in part because, for me, everything happens in the present. There's never a past, although sometimes I cheat my way to the future by inserting voy a (going to) before the infinitive form of a verb (Voy a aprender español - I am going to learn Spanish), but that's as far from the present as I venture. Why, after it became clear we'd be moving to Canada one day, probably, I told Sue, "I hoop ta pick up da Canadian faster, eh?"

<THWACK>

I have this soft spot on the side of my head…

While "they" say you should start learning a foreign language by finding a word you can own, I say, "Numbers first." Because when you own them, you can buy things you need, like food, clothing, and shelter. With the pricing gun having removed most of the fun of buying anything in "civilized" countries, if you're in a location like Ecuador, which often requires haggling, you can. Otherwise, you pay the first price instead of the final price.

In addition, because they're numbers, you already recognize them unless you've just moved to the United Arab Emirates, where the numbers sounded and looked different. So, after an Etisalat technician installed a landline telephone in my villa, I used the keypad to learn the numbers - what they looked like anyway.

The 1 (wahid) was easy because it looked like a 1. I owned it! But most of the rest took longer because the 2 (ithnan) looked like a backward 7. The 3 (thalaatha), like a backward 7, but with an extra squiggle on top. The 4 (arba'a), like an E. The 5 (khamsa), a 0. The 6 (sitta), a 7. The 7 (sab'a), a V. The 8 (thamaniya), an upside-down V. The 9 (tissa'a), a 9. I owned two numbers! And finally, the 0 ('ashra) looked like a decimal point.

Then, there was the decimal point and comma, reversed in Arabic.

"Mister John, where is the comma button on my calculator?" Real students. Real questions.

In case you were wondering, the only way to differentiate the decimal point (comma) from the zero that looked like one was their placement - the decimal point (comma) where you'd expect to find it, on the writing line, the zero pointed above it. At least my conversion confusion helped me understand the difficulties my Emirati students experienced doing math in English.

Before I moved to the UAE, I knew readers and writers of Arabic did so from right to left. What I didn't know but soon discovered was that readers and writers of Arabic numbers did so from left to right. Since my students were used to reading Arabic numbers in the opposite direction of Arabic text, some naturally assumed the same was true in English - text read and written left to right, but numbers right to left.

If you think math is difficult and don't know Arabic, try doing it in Arabic, and you'll know how my students felt. If you know Arabic, or even if you don't, try doing long division… with Roman numerals. I did, once, but I had to give up after the onset of an excruciating headache. It's one reason I have enormous respect for Roman architecture and engineering, knowing they managed to build the magnificent structures they did with the number system they had, one lacking a zero.

By learning Arabic numbers first, when I got my first paycheck from UAE University, printed in Arabic, I knew they were paying me the agreed-upon amount. Moreover, I knew it was my paycheck because I'd also learned to recognize my name in Arabic by then. And after putting on my big-boy pants, I learned to write my name in Arabic with the confidence that came from learning numbers first.

025

GO CALL YOUR MOTHER

If you've never seen the 1973 movie *The Paper Chase*, starring John Houseman as Professor Charles Kingsfield, go watch it, then come back and read the rest of this story. I'll wait. Really, it's not a problem. If you've seen the movie, you have a good idea of what Professor Kent Keegan was like... on a good day. While John Houseman was only acting (he won an Academy Award for his performance), Kent Keegan was not. He was the real deal, live, in person, and often in our faces.

Each year, a couple-two-three hundred students started at the University of Wisconsin-Milwaukee as would-be architects in the school's six-year (2+2+2) program that culminated in a Master of Architecture degree. The School of Architecture and Urban Planning (SARUP) admitted far fewer students to the second two-year block than the first, some of whom would be transfers from other universities, why the herd needed to be culled.

For the most part, Architectural Fundamentals 200, the first design course in SARUP, was the slaughterhouse for many aspiring architects at UWM. It was definitely not a warm and fuzzy, everyone gets a trophy, thanks for participating kind of class. Our section began with 30 or so students, but by the end of the semester, just over half remained, and some of them didn't return the following semester. While ARCH200 was the slaughterhouse, Professor Keegan, who taught most sections, was the butcher.

If brevity is the soul of lingerie, then Kent's design briefs were essentially nude because they contained almost no information or direction, students left bewildered, desperately wondering, "What does he want?" Kent was not forthcoming with direction, especially if you didn't know how to read between the lines, listen, or think. We could ask him questions at any time, but those who didn't think before inquiring paid a price because, in Kent's class, there were stupid questions.

Sure, he could've spoon-fed us with detailed design briefs, but then our projects would've merely reflected our skill at interpreting his instructions. By giving us as little direction as possible, he freed us to find our answers, not just guess at his, because he wanted to see what we could do. More importantly, he wanted us to see what we could do.

As a result, presentation days were unpredictable as hardly anyone's project looked like anyone else's, despite us all working off the same brief. To emphasize that point, one day, Kent distilled each student's design to a few representative lines and squiggles, creating an alphabet of sorts. No two were the same. Kent was quite pleased because it meant we'd all found our own solution.

We'd never know "the" answer because there never was one - designs just better or worse than others. Something that became crystal clear as we presented our solutions to the class and Professor Keegan. It wasn't easy standing beside our drawings in front of strangers -

137

the design process so profoundly personal. Every line we drew on our presentation boards displayed a little more of our soul for everyone to see.

Kent even made that difficult, as we had to draw all our projects on 20x30-inch white poster boards in black ink using technical pens. On the poster boards, we couldn't erase our mistakes or drips from failed pens, the smooth white surface porous enough to make the ink permanent. Once we made a mark, it was there for good. If we made a mistake, we could leave it for everyone to see or start over. The ink didn't dry immediately either, so if we weren't careful with our hands, not just the drawing one, we could smear the ink. Kent wanted us to think about every mark we made at a time when drawing skills mattered.

ARCH200 was the first studio design course for many of my classmates and me and our first experience presenting design work. On presentation days, the classroom resembled Easter Island, with everyone staring straight ahead. Silent. Motionless. Breathless. Often lacking in color. And it wasn't just the students, as Kent had the same stone-faced expression, offering no clue what he was thinking.

After each student presented, there was always an awkward silence before Kent would speak… he then leaving no doubt what he was thinking. None. A butcher would've marveled at his carving skills right down to the bone. Standing beside our latest design tacked to the wall, there was no place to hide. Why, to this day, when I see an example of bad design, I think, "Back in architecture school, we'd call that a long day."

Why I held a certain envy for students with other majors. Students who not only got a good night's sleep on a regular basis but passed or failed in relative obscurity. Bomb an economics exam? Who would know except for the student and the teaching assistant? Maybe the professor, possibly the parents. But in ARCH200, we saw what everyone designed, how they presented it, and how Kent critiqued it. For example...

"Hi, I'm Bob. Here's my project. This is my zone of entry. This is my zone of transition. This is my zone of gathering."

Kent responded, "Bob... care to expand?"

"This is my zone of entry... this is where you go in. This is my zone of transition... this is where you go from here to here. This is my zone of gathering... where you gather."

A not-impressed Kent inquired, "Bob, how long did you work on these drawings?"

"I don't know."

"20 hours? 30 hours? 40 hours?"

"30 hours. Yeah. About 30 hours."

"Bob, during those 30 hours you were working on these drawings, were you thinking about anything?"

"Yeah, I guess."

"Bob, would you please share with the class what you were thinking."

"OK. This is my zone of entry. You go in here because there's the entry... This is my zone of transition, so I put it between the entry and the gathering space... This is my zone of gathering because it's at the end of the transition."

Later that semester, after Kent provided us with a site plan - a topographical map - Bob arrived on presentation day with it taped, taped to his poster board. He'd drawn his design, in ink, over the plain paper topographical map.

When it was Bob's turn, an incredulous Kent asked, "Bob, why is your map taped to your poster board?"

"Because I couldn't draw it on the poster board."
"Why not?"
"Because it's impossible. How can I trace through cardboard?"
"Bob, look around the room... everyone else managed to transfer the topo map onto the poster board."

Bob had no answer.

"Sit down, Bob."

Bob didn't make it to the end of the semester, leaving on his own accord, finally demonstrating an understanding, of his situation anyway, thereby avoiding Kent's most cruel cut of all... "Here's a quarter. Go call your mother and tell her you're not going to be an architect." With that declaration and a flick of Kent's thumb, there was only the haunting sound of the bouncing coin on the laminated tabletop before it finally came to rest in front of the recipient. Whether it landed heads or tails mattered not, the student lost.

I saw dreams shattered that semester, wondering how many classmates declared an architecture major with little to no idea what an architect really does, given my peer group grew up with the likes of TV sitcom architects Wilbur Post and Mike Brady, neither with any real connection to reality. Movies weren't much better at accurately portraying architects, although the casting of Paul Newman as one in *The Towering Inferno* was brilliant!

If Professor Keegan ripping our designs apart, constructively, of course, wasn't difficult enough, some days, he brought his two sons to class. They'd sit on either side of him with their father's same stone-faced expression. We never knew what they were thinking either until Kent asked them for their opinion of a student's design. In some ways, his son's critiques were even more difficult to take because his sons... were still in grade school. Grade school! They hadn't even started paying for their education, yet there they were, critiquing our work, constructively, of course.

Humbling - when a grade-schooler gets it right, explaining how I got it wrong.

When Professor Keegan brought his sons to class, it wasn't to torment us further. It was simply his best option, some days his only option, Kent a single father. It was not his choice. It was not his wife's choice either. Years earlier, Kent heard the words no one wants to hear, "You have cancer." Those were followed by more words no one wants to hear, "You have six months. Start getting your affairs in order."

While Kent was doing that, his wife passed away unexpectedly. Professor Keegan suddenly found himself a widower with two young sons and a death sentence still hanging over his head. Much to the surprise of his doctors, Kent's cancer went into remission. He got a reprieve, a second chance at life. He was not about to waste a minute of it. He wouldn't allow students in his class to waste their time either... or his.

Kent's methods might sound cruel, but I figure he did many students a favor by pushing them out the door before they wasted any more time and money on a major they were wholly unsuited for. I hope Bob and others like him eventually came to that realization.

The intensity of Kent's class was more than some students could handle. There was no relief because everything in his class was a shared experience, including his handing out of grades. At the conclusion of presentation day, Kent and his teaching assistant, Guy, collected our drawings for further review. The next class, we'd arrive to find our graded boards propped up on the waist-high ledge along a side and the back wall of the room.

Our projects weren't randomly placed or arranged alphabetically. Instead, Kent and Guy put them in order, from best to worst, for everyone to see. While the syllabus and design briefs were opaque, the grading was transparent, as they placed the project they deemed the best next to the door, the worst in the far back corner. For the student whose project was in that corner, it was a long walk to collect their work, a walk some didn't make.

We didn't know it then, but as each project built upon the previous one, the only project that mattered was the final one. In the end, despite Kent's sometimes draconian methods, every misstep along the way could be forgiven because in Professor Keegan's Architectural Fundamentals 200 class, where we started mattered not. What did was where we finished.

If we finished.

026

THE EMPTY DESK

When I hear someone with no evidence of brain damage prattle on about how overpaid and underworked teachers are, I tell them, "You should quit your difficult, low-paying job and become a teacher. Let me know how that works out for you."

Try dealing with a career that requires a university degree and continuing education, yet high school dropouts collecting garbage are often better paid.

Try dealing with one of the few careers that requires a higher education, yet the only opportunity for advancement is to become an administrator, a completely different occupation.

Try dealing with some of those empire-building administrators, especially the ones who became administrators because teaching proved too difficult, didn't pay enough, or both.

Try dealing with a room full of students who bring their personalities and problems into your workspace every day for nine months, and then try teaching them something every day for nine months.

A long, long time ago, in a dorm room far away, I was watching TV talk show host Phil Donahue when he asked, more or less, "If I can present an hour-long show each day that fills a studio and gets ratings that keep me on the air, why can't teachers do a better job engaging their students?"

I liked Phil, but that day, I wanted to tell him off, to tell him, "Phil, you have only 44 minutes of airtime to fill each day. You have the rest of the day to prepare and staff to help you. You also get to choose whatever subject you want, a different one every day, the more titillating the better. You reportedly once told your staff, "I want all the topics hot." Fair enough, it's TV, but let's see you teach English grammar on your show. Every day. For nine months. Without the assistance of your staff. Tell me, Phil, how long would you still have an audience? Ratings? Or your TV show?"

One more thing, "Phil... try dealing with an empty desk. Just try." As a teacher, there was nothing more disturbing than the sight of an empty desk... that shouldn't be. This is just one of many issues teachers deal with, often not a part of their training, issues Ma could relate to as a teacher at Waupaca High School for 29 years. Why, after Ma retired, I know she enjoyed time spent in my classroom at Dubai Women's College - I bringing her to work a few times during her annual stay that could last a month or more.

She got to visit with my students, learn from them, and even teach them. She was fortunate because spending quality time with Emirati women was an opportunity not many Westerners got, even women. Moreover, my students appreciated the chance to talk to the mother of their (favorite) teacher, they happy that Ma, a former English teacher, could help them with what was often their most challenging subject.

Sometimes, students learn more when their teacher ignores the syllabus, something I learned from a former high school math teacher and my first boss in the UAE,

Tom. For my students, having the opportunity to interact with a visitor from the States was like taking a field trip without having to leave the classroom. I wasn't about to deny my students such an opportunity because of some syllabus I probably wasn't following closely anyway.

I told Ma she was to answer, truthfully, any questions my students asked, even when they asked about me - unless it were a question I wouldn't answer. I also told my students they could ask Ma whatever they wanted, promising I wouldn't ask her who asked what later. They knew I wouldn't, and I didn't.

One year, Ma chatted with one of my computer programming students. I knew Ma couldn't help her with that subject, and since this student's English was good, she didn't need any help there either. The two just seemed to connect. Because, for all the differences people tend to underscore when they barely see a woman dressed in black from a conservative Gulf country, if they ignore the packaging, they discover how much they have in common. If I learned anything in my nearly 15 years in the UAE, it's that people are people, especially with society's labels removed.

After class ended, Ma stayed behind and continued her conversation with the student. Everyone went home happy that Thursday - by then, the government had changed the weekend to Friday/Saturday from Thursday/Friday, just when I was finally getting used to Wednesday being Friday.

The following Saturday night, I received a phone call from a friend and former student of mine at UAE University, Mariam Al Shamsi. She told me she'd encountered a horrible car crash on the highway between Dubai and her hometown of Fujairah - six members of one family were killed. One casualty was a

Dubai Women's College student, but Mariam didn't know her name. When I told Ma about the accident, I explained that there were over 2000 students at the Dubai Women's College, so odds were this student was not one of mine.

Shortly after I arrived at work on Sunday, I learned the name Mariam did not know. "I have a student named…" There were many repeats since Emiratis went by their given name and their father's name. In a class of 25 at UAE University, I once had seven students named Maryam Mohammed. Seven. So surely this was the case, just another student with the same name, but I had to know, making my way to her homeroom.

Knocking on the door to announce my imminent entrance, giving the ladies time to cover themselves if need be, I hoped the student in question would be the first I'd see. But after opening the door, the expressions I saw, and the student I didn't, told me the accident victim was not another student with the same name. She was my student.

Standing in the doorway, still hoping it wasn't so, I pointed to her empty desk. The students nodded. I stepped back as I gathered my face, closing the door behind me, leaving my students to mourn their classmate. No walk back to my office was ever longer.

Later, when I returned for my regularly scheduled class… let's say I didn't stick to the syllabus that day either, but I know everyone learned more, including me, than if I had. It was a difficult hour, probably more than any Phil Donahue ever dealt with on his show. Worse yet, worse than even the drive home that Sunday evening in Dubai's horrendous rush hour traffic, I knew after I arrived, I'd have to tell Ma that the student she'd chatted with for so long Thursday afternoon… was in the car… and not her desk.

027

OUTSIDE THE BOX

Overlooking the river valleys and downtown core, the building where I was born is now home to the Eau Claire Academy. Situated on wooded grounds in a quiet residential neighborhood on the city's north side, since 1967, this co-ed campus has provided treatment for young people experiencing one or more of the following characteristics:

- Emotional Disorders
- Educational Difficulties
- Impaired Social Relationships
- Dual Diagnosis with Drug or Alcohol Abuse
- Behavioral Disturbances
- Psychiatric Disorders

Some would say I should never have left the building after Ma gave birth to me there, in 1962, when it was Sacred Heart Hospital, the new Sacred Heart Hospital opening in 1966 on the city's south side.

Still next door to the Eau Claire Academy is Sacred Heart Church. Built in 1928, the enormous red brick building has been on the National Register of Historic Places since 1983. Added for its architectural significance, the only architectural elements that mattered to any kid in the neighborhood were the church's towering twin steeples, that, after dark, creeped the bajeezzuzz out of us, especially with all the bats in the belfry flying about.

"You know they got a guy nailed to the wall in there."

I don't recall there being a guy nailed to the wall, what with Ma and me being excommunicated from the Catholic Church before I was old enough to spit up solid food. This despite her writing a letter to the Pope… about the excommunication thing, not my spitting up solid food. There were other churches, so Ma had options, including not going to any.

When she was pregnant with me, she also had options, as she could've gone to Luther Hospital in downtown Eau Claire. However, in my next hometown, she would've had no choice as most children born in Waupaca since 1954 had their coming-out party in the town's only hospital, Riverside. Many of my classmates, like Dan, the first friend I made after moving to Waupaca in 1971, were born there. And in an odd bit of asymmetrical symmetry, most lifelong Waupaca residents will make the same journey, from Riverside to Lakeside, the town's only cemetery, located just upstream (seems like it should be downstream) from Riverside.

Residents had more in common than just their place of birth, Waupaca located in that tiny pocket of the States that refers to drinking fountains as bubblers. Area residents had more than just uncommon vocabulary in common as well, given the many with Nordic heritage, seemingly everyone's last name ending in "son" or "sen," the alternate spellings providing a dash of diversity.

Dan, whose family name ends in "son," still lives in Waupaca. He married Marsha, from the other side of the county, the pair raising two daughters as owners of the ever-popular Waupaca Woods Restaurant. Mostly because as long as I've known Waupaca, it's always included Dan, so I can't imagine him living elsewhere. I hope he stays there because he seems happy right where he is, and until he retires, I'll have a great place to eat whenever I'm in town.

But I couldn't imagine living in Waupaca or anywhere else my entire life. From the time I saw those jets flying overhead while standing in Bob and Susie's backyard, I knew there was more out there, and I wanted to see it, experience it, live it. So it's no surprise that Google Earth is one of my favorite computer applications because I can almost see the world without leaving my desk.

I can also go for a "drive" in numerous locations worldwide using GE's Street View. "Oh, so that's what Dildo, Newfoundland, looks like. Somehow... I expected... something else..." Years later, though, when I saw it for myself, I thought it was a charming little town, perhaps a nice place to live.

Sue and I use the application to check out real estate in places we might consider moving to, like Dildo. If Street View is available, all the better, as we can be looky-loos without leaving home. We've saved a lot of time and money not traveling to see properties we wouldn't have purchased had we gone. Sue and I even used GE to scout the location for our wedding ceremony. Believe it, Google sent one of their camera cars down the dead-end (paved) road to the tiny town of Calico Basin, Nevada.

Then there are all the photos posted online, especially since smartphone cameras came along. This must be the first time in history photos outnumber ants, and that's only counting selfies. The result? It's never been easier to see so much without actually going anywhere. Nevertheless, even the best digital imagery is no substitute for a boots-on-the-ground perspective because they're only images.

While I've tried, I've never been able to explain (to my satisfaction) why even extended travel is not anywhere close to the experience of living in another country. There's just so much to see, so much to experience, so much to learn, especially if the culture is a far different one. Why I never felt so ignorant as I did my first year living in Al Ain. There was so much I didn't know, so many people who knew more than me yet still didn't know it all. Why I don't consider myself an expert on expat living, even after so many years, because there's still so much I don't know and know I never will.

Still naive, at the end of my first year in the United Arab Emirates, I sent letters, 26 pages long, to family and friends describing my experiences living there. After another year in Al Ain, I had to correct myself a few times because some of what I initially thought was true was not. I needed more time to get to know the feel of another culture's fabric.

So, for the most part, I stopped trying to explain, accepting that it's one of those things that can only be learned. Five years into our life near Vilcabamba, I got some confirmation of this after a woman who wrote a travel blog with a readership approaching double digits harpooned the town as a great place to live based on her three-day stay.

"It rains all the time!"

Well, yes, she was in town during the rainy season when it did indeed rain three days in a row. She did some "research," discovering the rainy season in Vilcabamba ran from October to March, and in her tiny mind, the only conclusion she could draw was that it must rain for six months, the same as she experienced during her short stay. It did not.

She also based her impressions of the local expat population on those she encountered in the town square. There were hundreds of gringos living in the area, but the dozen or so hanging about the square were enough for her to declare that every expat in Vilcabamba was an old, drunken hippie. They were not.

The rest of her report was just as inaccurate, a local gringo realtor trying, and failing, to convince her of that. I didn't bother, having already learned my lesson. Besides, what did I know? At the time, I'd only lived in the Vilcabamba area for five years. Despite all I learned in my nearly 15 years in the UAE, I knew I left with even more to learn.

While family and friends asked questions about the UAE when I traveled to the States during my summer breaks, I received far fewer than expected. Everything about the UAE was so foreign to them that many didn't know what to ask. And then there's the fear too many have of asking a stupid question, preferring to remain ignorant rather than appear so.

Back in Waupaca one summer, I ran into a former classmate and still a good friend, who, I'm happy to say, asked questions. During our conversation, Julie (her family name ends with "son") remarked that she couldn't imagine living in the UAE.

"I didn't like the few months I spent living just 40 miles away in Appleton!"

Why she moved back to Waupaca, where she was born, at Riverside Hospital.

Many wouldn't want the life I have. I get that. I know my life would've been much different had I never left Eau Claire, Waupaca, Wisconsin, or the States, but then I would've missed the life I have, one I wouldn't trade for anything, even though it's nothing like what I envisioned. As I tell anyone who asks, expat life isn't better or worse. It's just different.

And then there's my friend, Brenda, quoted on the back cover of this book, who was aware, maybe more than I was at the time, that my life was somewhere down the road less traveled. Even so, if anyone had told me how so many years and so many miles would've exposed me to what it has, I wouldn't have believed it.

Still on the road less traveled, I have no idea where I'll be when my road "dead ends," but I don't want to wind up in a cemetery, six feet under, sealed in a box. Instead, assuming the manner of my death allows, I want to be cremated, my ashes spread in places like Eau Claire, Haida Gwaii, Vilcabamba, Sharjah, Al Ain, Dubai, the Red Rock area west of Las Vegas, Waupaca's Chain O'Lakes, Newfoundland, and maybe a place or two I haven't been... yet. Because, even in death, I want to be outside the box so I get around, same as when I was alive.

028

T.4.I.W.

Jeremy Williams wrote a book entitled Don't They Know It's Friday? - Cross Cultural Considerations for Business and Life in the Gulf. The subtitle is self-explanatory, but the title, not so much, unless you've read the book or worked in the Gulf.

Williams probably called it the Gulf because, on the south side, the Arab side - Bahrain, Kuwait, Oman, Qatar, Saudi Arabia, and the United Arab Emirates - that particular body of water was known as the Arabian Gulf, but on the north side, the Persian side - Iran - it was the Persian Gulf.

The book's title referred to a problem that would arise because countries on both sides of the Gulf had a different workweek than most of the world. When those in Western countries called a business in the Gulf, they often wondered, "Why is nobody answering the telephone?"

"Because it's Friday!"

Just as Sunday was the day for Christians to go to church, Friday was the day for Muslims to go to the mosque, a day when most businesses were closed. So when I worked in the UAE, Saturday, once my favorite day, became my least, the first of the workweek.

Monday became hump day (Monday just can't win), while Wednesday was promoted to T.A.I.W. - Thank Allah It's Wednesday, the last day of the workweek.

It might seem like a minor adjustment, but it took more getting used to than you might think. Even after a few years of experience, I still got confused, especially when it came to scheduling. The workweek shift was just one of those things I had to deal with as an expat.

Another difference was that the UAE also used the Islamic calendar, which began in 622 AD, the year the Prophet Muhammad and his followers migrated from Mecca to Medina, where they established the first Muslim community, an event known as the Hijra. In the Gregorian calendar, years are referenced as "AD" - Anno Domini, Latin for the year of the Lord, but in the Islamic calendar, years are "AH" - after the Hijra.

Based on 28 or 29-day lunar cycles, the Islamic calendar was significantly different. Nothing matched - not the days, months, or years, and thus, the date was foreign. Some things were familiar. Weeks were still seven days. At 28 or 29 days, every month was like February. And a year was still 12 months, even though it was based on the moon, not the sun.

Mainly used to establish religious holidays, the Islamic calendar had little impact on my day-to-day life - I only noticing what day it was when reading the local newspapers that listed both the Islamic date and Gregorian date. Only during the month of Ramadan did the Islamic calendar matter to me because the government mandated a shorter workday for both government and non-government employees.

My first year in the UAE, with a favorable schedule during Ramadan, I popped in to teach classes for four consecutive periods, then went home. Two solid hours of work. By the end of Ramadan, I'd worked a paltry

36 hours but still got paid my usual monthly salary. That perk was one reason why Ramadan was my favorite month. Because the Islamic calendar is based on lunar cycles, each year only 354 or 355 days instead of 365, it "backed up" relative to the Gregorian calendar. Fortunately, for the nearly 15 years I taught in the UAE, Ramadan always fell during the school year.

One year, near the end of Ramadan, the government announced that every government employee would get paid, twice, UAE President His Highness Shaikh Zayed bin Sultan al Nahyan feeling particularly generous. Having heard rumors of the coming double payday, believe it, some colleagues complained, thinking they were only getting their base salary, not their full salary, which included a housing and transportation allowance.

"Just shut up and say, "Shukran" (thank you), you ungrateful bastard."

We did indeed get our full salaries.

"Shukran, Shaikh Zayed!"

But it was really only the staggered workweek that was an issue. Just when I got used to the two-day shift, summer break would roll around, and I'd head back to North America - where T.G.I.F. made sense - and I'd get all messed up again. I likened it to visiting family or friends in a city with a different cable TV system and having to learn a new lineup of channels - all there, just not in the same place.

Eventually, I became comfortable with what day was what in which hemisphere... just in time for the UAE government to change the weekend from Thursday/Friday to Friday/Saturday. Sunday was now Monday, Tuesday was hump day, Friday was still Sunday because prayer day at the mosque didn't change, Saturday was Saturday, except that it came after Sunday, and I didn't know what day it was... again. There was no Daylight Saving Time in the UAE, though, so...

Only one day different from what I knew in the States, I found the adjustment even more difficult because the new workweek... wasn't different enough. The only way the Emirati government could've confused me more was by making the workweek exactly the same because I probably would've kept converting days even when I didn't need to.

After nearly 15 years of that, I moved to Ecuador. Ah, Ecuador, where Monday was Monday, Friday was Friday, Sunday was Sunday... and again, no Daylight Saving Time. Excellent. Really. Except in most of Latin America, the weekend was Saturday/Sunday.

"But John, that's the same as the States."

Yes, but in Latin America, calendars accurately reflect the weekend, with Monday being the first day of the week, so Saturday and Sunday come at the end of the week - the weekend. Imagine that. While that made sense, it's amazing how innocuous things like a calendar ingrain the order of days into your brain. Because if you're like me, when you look at a calendar without actually reading it, you think Sunday is the first day of the week, Saturday the last, with Wednesday smack in the middle.

The only time it was an issue was when I booked flights online with Latin American air carriers, their calendars in the regional format - Monday to Sunday instead of Sunday to Saturday. A couple of times, I almost booked flights a day later than I wanted to. Almost.

Now retired, so every day is a holiday, I no longer care what the calendar says, mostly because I no longer care what day it is, other than it's today, as Winnie the Pooh said, "...my favorite day."

Just an FYI - Before I began living the expat life and knew no other workweek or calendar, I still had to stop and think about what day it was once football season was over. So there's that…

029

WHO WAS THE NOVELTY

Growing up in Eau Claire, there wasn't much color in my life, what with our one-channel, 13-inch black-and-white Motorola TV. Even if we'd gotten as many channels as our aerialed neighbors, Bob and Susie, they still would've been in black-and-white. Well, mostly white because even as TV transitioned to color, most people on it lacked any.

The only real ethnic diversity I encountered came while watching sports. Basketball, in particular, as Ma took me to many a game at Zorn Arena on the University of Wisconsin-Eau Claire campus, entertainment she could afford as a single mother and a UWEC student, entitled to free admission.

In the bandbox built for basketball, the game atmosphere was good and loud because the Blugolds, coached by Ken Anderson, were one of the best non-scholarship programs in the country, almost always sending the home fans home happy, so often, I thought the home team was supposed to win every game.

Along with Blugolds games, I saw diversity in the college and professional basketball I watched on TV. I would not see a high school game in person until Ma got her first teaching job at Waupaca High School.

When basketball season bounced around, Ma and Del took me to a game, the first I'd seen in person somewhere other than Zorn Arena.

Located downtown, the old Waupaca High School gymnasium was a similar but smaller version of the only basketball venue I'd ever known. Overhead was a tangle of silver-painted steel trusses and sheet metal air ducts. Below was a beautiful hardwood floor with so many painted-on lines for sports other than basketball, it looked like an early work of Piet Mondrian, not that I knew who Mondrian was, then, but I'd learn. Two years later, in fifth grade, I'd learn the games those lines were for, never before having a physical education class in a proper gym.

On the east and west sides, retractable wooden bleachers fronted the lower half of concrete block walls painted a hideous "kids been peeing in the pool green," befitting the school colors, blue and white. Mounted high on the south wall, west side, was a Longines scoreboard, the Swiss manufacturer's name appearing just above the game clock - I thinking Longines a fancy adult word for how long before a quarter was over.

At the north end was something Zorn Arena didn't have - a wood-framed stage with a red brick base where the pep band played. Directed by "Buzz" Hoeffer, they got the gym jumping before the opening tip.

What it lacked in color correctness, the gym more than made up for in character, underscoring everything good about small-town basketball. Taxpayers have since paid for two new high schools, but neither gym in either replacement matched the old one. This was especially true of the gym in the cardboard box iteration I attended featuring a brown rubber floor and lemon-yellow roof trusses and ductwork. Yes, the school colors were still blue and white.

For my first high school basketball game, I sat to the right of Ma, who sat to the right of Del, a few rows behind the Waupaca bench. Coach Colbert wanted faculty to sit there to provide a buffer between his team and any fans of the opposing team. Before the pre-game warm-ups, with a popcorn box in hand, I enjoyed Buzz's band, "Ma, we should get some drums!" I found the cheerleaders almost as entertaining, not that I knew why, then, but I'd learn.

With Buzz's band belting out their stirring rendition of *Jesus Christ Superstar*, the energy was there, but the players were not. But when the band struck up the school fight song, "Here comes the blue and the white..." because "Here comes the kids been peeing in the pool green..." doesn't rhyme with the song's next line, "Ready tonight to put up a fight..." the home team finally emerged from the locker room, down and to my right. As they passed, I was puzzled. Looking for answers, I turned to Ma.

"Where are the black guys?"

With the innocence of the child I was, I wanted to know because, in my nine years, I'd never seen an all-white team. Because in Waupaca, in Waupaca County, then one of the least ethnically diverse counties in the States, almost everyone looked a lot like me, even though many residents had Nordic heritage, and I did not. The lack of diversity in my new home of Waupaca took some getting used to.

A few years later, lagging behind TV's transition to color, a couple of Mexican families moved into our neighborhood on Lawson Drive. Good people, their welcome presence inspired me to study Spanish in high school, where I'd get a taste of my life to come during a field trip to Mexico where no one, except my classmates, looked like me.

Years later, attending universities in Gainesville, Milwaukee, and even Platteville, to a degree, I encountered diversity on a regular basis. Nevertheless, only after moving to the United Arab Emirates would I appreciate that it was not a person of color but me who was the novelty.

030

KEVIN BACON LOOKS JUST LIKE YOU

It happens. Someone I've not yet met telling me, "You look just like Kevin Bacon!" then maybe saying, "Hello," and introducing themselves. It happens more often than I think it should because I don't see a "remarkable" resemblance.

Those who do cross cultural and geographic boundaries, from students at United Arab Emirates University in Al Ain to an American woman in an elevator at the Red Rock Hotel & Casino in Las Vegas, where they all told me, "You look just like Kevin Bacon!" Just once, I'd like a stranger to say to me, "Kevin Bacon looks just like you!" or ask, "Are you Kevin Bacon?" because maybe I am.

I don't mind the comparisons, as the highly respected British daily newspaper, The Guardian, named Kevin one of the best actors never to receive an Academy Award nomination. He's also multitalented, with director and musician included in his lengthy resume. Mostly, I don't mind because Kevin strikes me as a good guy, someone I'd invite over for a barbecue, along with his wife, actress Kyra Sedgwick. The two have been married since 1988, which qualifies as an eternity for a Hollywood couple.

Once strangers have compared me to my doppelgänger, I can't help but think of the parlor game, Six Degrees of Kevin Bacon, based on the six degrees of separation concept that no more than six acquaintances separate any two people. So, pick a person, any person, and, at most, you know someone who knows someone who knows someone who knows someone who knows someone who knows someone who knows them - remarkable, and scary, considering who's out there.

In Six Degrees of Kevin Bacon, participants assign themselves, or others, a Bacon Number based on how many degrees of separation they have from the celebrity. Kevin has a Bacon Number of 0 because he's Kevin Bacon. Anyone with a direct connection with him, like his wife, has a Bacon Number of 1. Those who don't have a direct connection with Kevin but have one with someone who does have a Bacon Number of 2, and so on. Just seeing someone doesn't count. The two people have to meet and at least greet, making a connection so each knows of the other's existence.

For example, in June 2019, I saw Paul McCartney in concert at Green Bay's Lambeau Field from the 35th row. So, while I was very aware of Paul's presence, to him, at best, I was just another face in the crowd. Rod Stewart and I have a connection, although one he surely doesn't remember, because we did the meet and greet thing as we browsed opposite sides of the same magazine rack in London's Heathrow Airport.

To the best of my knowledge, my Bacon Number is 3. So how do I get that? By having a Rod Stewart Number of 1 - he in the 1998 movie *54* with Neve Campbell, who was in the 1998 movie *Wild Things* with Kevin Bacon.

If anyone I've met ever met Kevin, my Bacon Number would drop to 2, the lowest it could be without the two of us meeting - if there are two of us. If Kevin and I should meet, I know how I will greet, "You look just like John Curran!" then I'll say, "Hello" and introduce myself, see what he says, and if Kyra is with him, see what she says.

If you think it far-fetched that no one has more than six degrees of separation from Kevin Bacon or anyone else, consider this... I'm just a guy, but there's only one degree of separation between me and Queen Elizabeth II, Fidel Castro, Saddam Hussain, Richard Nixon, Pierre Trudeau, John F. Kennedy, George H.W. Bush, Bill Clinton, Indira Gandhi, Mikhail Gorbachev, Margaret Thatcher, Vladimir Putin, Xi Jinping, Muammar al Qaddafi, Nelson Mandela, and Golda Meir - only two degrees then separating me from anyone they've met. See? Remarkable, and scary, considering who's out there.

That little ole me is so well connected makes me think there's something to this six degrees concept because I know people who've never left Wisconsin, but because they've met me, no more than two people separate them from all those world leaders. That's how connected we are, and partly why it's so easy for a pandemic to spread, especially with air travel commonplace, which helped bring Sir Rodney and me together.

Besides the obvious, I hope Kevin and I meet so we can talk about six degrees, he on the record saying, "If you take me out of it, I find six degrees to be a beautiful concept we should try to live by. It's about compassion and responsibility for everyone on the planet." A concept I came to appreciate after moving to the UAE - teaching students from Morocco to Indonesia, dating women from Sudan to Sri Lanka, and working and living with expats from around the world.

Once I saw how the dots connected, I no longer saw disaster, war, famine, poverty, or sanctions affecting anonymous people but someone I knew... or someone they knew... or someone they knew... Why, in July 2006, it was difficult for me to sit across from some good ole boys watching CNN at an Atlanta airport departure gate, delighting in the destruction as clips aired of the Israeli military bombing Lebanon.

It was particularly difficult because those bombed included friends and colleagues home on their summer break. While Sue and I were enjoying the adventure of a lifetime, making our first trip to Haida Gwaii and then Ecuador, where we purchased our acre-and-a-half of dream-come-true, a colleague and friend of mine, Hala, was "vacationing" with her family in a Beirut bomb shelter, while a colleague of Sue's saw their house blown to bits... fortunately from the outside, not the inside.

While I, too, find six degrees to be a beautiful concept we should try to live by, I can only imagine the reaction I would've received had I tried to explain that to those good ole boys. Sensing I was about to spray the verbal version of the water hose that got away from me at Beerworld in Gainesville - Sue not so gently reminded me I was in an American airport where she didn't want security regarding me as a troublemaker.

Knowing Sue was right, again, I grudgingly bit my tongue as the pair continued spraying their prejudice, demonstrating an utter lack of compassion for the anonymous bombing victims they saw on TV, some losing everything they had, including their lives. Yet, with Sue and I sitting within spitting distance (I was tempted), those good ole boys, unbeknownst to them, had fewer degrees of separation from some of those victims than I had from Kevin Bacon.

165

031

I'VE BEEN TO ELVIS' HOUSE

I've never been one to hover around a celebrity, hoping for an autograph, a selfie, or a chance to kill them. But one time, during a family vacation with Ma and Del, I found myself at the gates of Graceland, Elvis Presley's home in Memphis, Tennessee. That brush with the home of greatness led to an unexpected verbal exchange years later just north of Al Ain at the Hili Fun City ice rink.

Growing up in Wisconsin, where frozen water was everywhere in the winter, sometimes the late fall, or the early spring, occasionally the early fall, or the late spring... but never in summer, I had no excuse for not knowing how to ice skate, yet I didn't know. Just because I didn't know how to ice skate didn't mean I never went skating. I just wouldn't call what I did skating, even though I wore skates.

That's because Jay and his friends liked to play "crack the whip," especially after a few beers. If you're unfamiliar with such winter fun - crack the whip, not beer-drinking - skaters would join hands, forming a line as they skated. Once the line was long enough, the head of the line would veer, causing the tail of the line to swing around rapidly.

When the "whip" cracked, those on the tail end would fly across the ice until gravity, friction, a snow bank, a fence, unsuspecting skaters, or some other obstacle stopped them. Always positioned at the tail end of the whip, my lack of skating ability mattered not. I only needed to be willing and durable. Probably didn't even need the skates.

Enjoying my time as a human hockey puck, I never learned to ice skate properly until that night at the Hili Fun City ice rink in the desert on the edge of the Empty Quarter of the Arabian Peninsula because… where else would a Wisconsin boy learn?

Fun City. The name probably lost something in the translation, like those (poorly) translated foreign commercials spouting a multitude of superlatives or foreign businesses that try to attract tourists with names like "The Most Exotic Marigold Hotel." With the name Fun City, I just knew it'd be a letdown, and it was because it wasn't fun, not by American standards.

Outside the arena, there were some kiddie carnival rides, but other than that, there wasn't much fun to be had, for adults anyway. And concessions? What are those? The place had the look of a carnival on the verge of bankruptcy. But that's how it was in Al Ain in 1991 - we had to make our fun in the days before satellite TV, the Internet, shopping malls, and English-language movie theaters. So we threw a lot of parties, moving from villa to villa every week to keep the neighbors and the authorities guessing.

Otherwise, going out mainly meant going out to eat - restaurants were everywhere - because outside the two major hotels, the Hilton and the InterContinental, there was little else to do. Why, for most Westerners, the hotels were entertainment hubs because there were swimming pools, gyms, tennis courts, discos, and more restaurants, along with bars where alcohol could be served and consumed legally. The InterCon also hosted rugby matches, as it was then one of the few places in the UAE with a grass pitch (field).

The hotels also booked live entertainment, primarily up-and-coming or over-the-hill bands and belly dancers. For a few years, there was even dinner theatre in Al Ain, the InterCon bringing in traveling productions, always British, to perform in the hotel's ballroom. Considering the venue, they were quality performances. I even recognized some cast members from public television shows I saw in the States.

My enjoyment was somewhat dampened when I learned the performers weren't always as happy to be in Al Ain as I was. Reading an early '90s interview with actor Patrick Macnee, star of the iconic British TV series *The Avengers*, he mentioned the low of his career, occurring years before the UAE boom.

"I've seen the nadir. I've done dinner theatre in Abu Dhabi."

Abu Dhabi? The nadir? Apparently, he never did dinner theatre in Al Ain or a children's program at Hili Fun City.

The Fun City ice rink looked much like any ice rink in the States or Canada, except for the massive portrait of His Highness Shaikh Zayed bin Sultan al Nahyan, then President of the United Arab Emirates, mounted on the back wall at center ice. As I went slip-sliding around the rink, I felt like Big Brother was watching my every floundering move.

The "morality police" were probably watching as well because I was there with three unmarried women, all under 25 years of age - a teacher and a teaching assistant, both from the States, and a nurse from England. I thought the nurse might be helpful since I didn't know how to skate, but I soon discovered that the local guys were more than willing to teach me and help keep me from falling.

While I appreciated their efforts, they also had an agenda that soon became apparent because what they really wanted was to know whether any of the ladies with me were my sister and whether they were "available." None of the ladies came close to looking like a sister of mine, but to them, I guess we all looked "same same." So even before I hit the ice, literally, they were already befriending me.

As I laced up my rented skates, one Emirati boy, 16 or so years old, struck up a conversation in his best broken English…

"Hello."
"Hello."
"What your name?"
"John."
"American?"
"Yes."
"Know Elvis Presley?"
"Yes. I've been to Elvis' house."
"YOU BEEN TO ELVIS' HOUSE!"

I'll never forget the astonished look on his face - his eyes owl-wide, his mouth resembling that of a bottom-feeding fish. Given his reaction, I think he thought I sat around and shot out TV screens with The King while downing deep-fried peanut butter, bacon, and banana sandwiches.

Sure, I could've clarified my "relationship" with Elvis, but I didn't, I couldn't. The boy was so happy to know someone who knew Elvis, someone with an Elvis Number of 1, how could I tell him I didn't know Elvis the way he misunderstood I did? How could I tell him the closest I ever got to Elvis was standing at the gates of

Graceland, watching my mother scribble her telephone number on the stone wall surrounding America's second most famous residence?

The King was home that day, but Ma told me he never called. Elvis died a month later... it was in all the papers.

032

MY MOTHER GETS AROUND

I never met Flossy Floozy, an over-the-top character Ma portrayed for mock job interviews to help her students at Waupaca High School with their real ones. I never met Flossy because Ma stopped playing the part once I became one of those students. With me in the building and my friends in her classroom, she didn't want to embarrass me, even though I would've laughed along with everyone else.

From the name, you can guess what Flossy Floozy was about. For her October 1977 "interview" with high-school-guidance-counselor-turned-potential-boss for the day, Court Dillingham, Ma dressed for the part in a turquoise, green, and gold sleeveless brocade sheath her mother made for her for a New Year's Eve party. Oversized, black plastic-framed sunglasses hid her eyes, a big string of fake pearls hung around her neck, there was a long, purposeful run in her nylons, and hot pink fuzzy slippers, given to her by Del for a hospital stay when she had her gall bladder removed, covered her feet. She also stuffed her mouth with a wad of chewing gum for blowing bubbles at "appropriate" times.

While Flossy got around in one way, Ma got around in another. Her first trip to a foreign country was in July 1966, to Canada, just across the border from Grand Marais, Minnesota, on the north shore of Lake Superior. This was also my and my Grandma Curran's first trip to another country. Ma's first big trip was to the Union of Soviet Socialist Republics (U.S.S.R.) in March 1969, when Americans regarded the country as the world's bogeyman. While she was away, I got around, staying with various family and friends until her return two weeks later.

Just six (and a half!) years old, I didn't understand the geopolitics, but I knew from the reactions of the adults around me that her trip was a big deal. I also sensed some fear for her safety, why I was happy she returned… with goodies for me. The babushka dolls were unlike anything I'd ever seen, and already a coin collector, the funny money she brought back was worth a fortune, to me anyway. I was particularly enamored with the Danish quarter-sized coins with a hole in the middle. Then I saw her slide show, a glimpse of what was so far away people needed to fly.

In the '70s, Ma, Del, and I took annual summer driving trips around the States and Canada. As a result, I'd traveled to over 40 states and five provinces before I ever made it to Milwaukee, which, oddly enough, didn't happen until I was 17, the same day I took my first ever airplane ride, on a Cessna, with my Uncle David at the controls. In the '80s, Ma and Del continued their driving trips without me. As Captain of the Chief Waupaca, I was lucky to get a day off, most of my summers spent within earshot of the authentic stern wheel paddleboat's air horn.

After I moved to Al Ain in July 1991, Ma made a trip to the United Arab Emirates in 1993, when tourism there was all but illegal. The amount of paperwork required just to get her into the country was staggering and expensive, and then again after we returned from a side trip to Egypt. On the way back to the States, we stopped in Paris for a few days, my second time there, her first. For Ma, after experiencing the pre-boom UAE and then Egypt, those countries so unlike the States, Paris was a bit of a letdown.

"It's almost like being back in the States."

"Next time, we'll go to Paris first."

"Next time."

We'd travel together again over Y2K, the University of Wisconsin football team playing in the Rose Bowl on New Year's Day 2000. While I managed to procure a couple of tickets for the game, all the flights to Los Angeles were booked by then, so we flew to Las Vegas instead, staying at the Luxor for a few days before driving a rented car to Los Angeles on December 30th. We spent the day at a relatively deserted Universal Studios on New Year's Eve, Badgers fans seemingly the only ones willing to brave the cold and rainy weather.

On New Year's Day, Y2K not ending the world as we knew it, we drove to Pasadena to watch the Rose Parade before making our way to the Rose Bowl for the football game. Wisconsin beat Stanford 17-9, but almost as entertaining was the one Stanford fan in our section driven bonkers by Badgers fans' "Rooooooon DAYNE!" cheer every time the Heisman Trophy winner touched the ball. After the game, we drove back to Vegas and donated a few more bucks to the slots before flying back to Wisconsin.

After I moved back to the UAE in 2001, Ma made yearly trips there. By then, the country had decided tourism was good and good for business. In contrast to the hassle and hundreds of dollars it cost to get Ma's visa in 1993, after the UAE's change in attitude, she paid just $27 for an instant visa upon arrival.

Inside her trips to the UAE, Sue and I scheduled another trip over our semester break so we could travel together to relatively out-of-the-way places Ma most likely wouldn't have visited from North America, such as Kenya, Sri Lanka, Turkey, and Oman. Ma also traveled to Ecuador a few times after Sue and I bought our property there in July 2006, then moved there in July 2007.

After she retired from teaching in June 2000, Ma made many more trips after Holiday Travel in Eau Claire hired her as a tour manager. For 15 years, longer than I think even she expected, she escorted numerous groups on tours in North America and Europe while using her employee discount to go on others as a customer. In the '10s, after retiring from Holiday, she still traveled, mainly with a younger sister, Ruth. The highlight was the two traveling to Russia 49 years after Ma's visit to the U.S.S.R.

In 2019, after making my first trip to the States in six years, I took Ma on a short trip to Green Bay's Lambeau Field for a Paul McCartney concert. Probably the last concert she'll ever attend, it made a great bookend to her first, Buddy Holly, in Eau Claire, days before he died in a plane crash. Then I took her on another, longer one, longer than even our summer driving trips as we traveled from Wisconsin to Haida Gwaii and back, a journey of some 7000 miles.

I thought that would probably be her last big trip. Ma was not as young as she used to be, and then COVID hit, denying her any opportunity to travel if she felt up to it. Early in 2022, though, I asked if she was up for one more road trip, to Newfoundland, the only Canadian province she hadn't been to. She was. By the time we returned from yet another 7000-mile journey, not only had she been to every province, I had too, also adding three more states to my list, leaving only three yet to visit.

Even if she doesn't take any more trips, especially those requiring a passport, she'll still get around, reviewing her photos, postcards, and extensive notes from all her trips. There's plenty of each as not only has she been to all 50 states and every Canadian province, but she's also been to Mexico, Costa Rica, Ecuador, Ireland, Northern Ireland, Wales, Scotland, England, Denmark, Finland, Latvia, Lithuania, Estonia, Ukraine, Netherlands, Belgium, France, Monaco, Spain, Portugal, Switzerland, Liechtenstein, Germany, Poland, Italy, Czech Republic, Austria, Slovenia, Croatia, Bosnia, Serbia, Hungary, Romania, Bulgaria, Slovakia, Australia, New Zealand, Egypt, Morocco, Kenya, Oman, Turkey, Sri Lanka, China, the U.S.S.R., Russia, and the United Arab Emirates, some more than once.

Ma says my moving to the UAE inspired her to travel more, which makes me smile. What puts an even bigger smile on my face is that while she's lived her whole life in Wisconsin, she's traveled far more than I have and probably ever will, even though I've lived over half my life and counting in the Middle East and South America. So when I think of Ma, my first thought is that even more than Flossy Floozy… my mother gets around.

033

I KNOW THERE BEFORE I AM

No thinking. No looking. Without hesitation… point to the northwest. OK, now find out what direction you pointed. How'd you do? If you nailed it, you might be one of those people with a good sense of direction and built-in GPS, like me, with no batteries or satellites required. Having a good sense of direction is one of those things for which I'm grateful. It's not something I learned. It's not something I was taught. I think it's one of those things a person has or hasn't, one I'm sure has made it easier for me to navigate life, and not just in a directional sense.

I find confidence in always knowing where I am, especially when I shouldn't. Like the night I piloted the Chief Waupaca in the dark and fog so thick I couldn't see much beyond the sternwheeler's bow. For four hours, on wits alone, I navigated narrow channels, sandbars, docks, rafts, a few ducks, and a couple of other crazy boaters without incident while over 100 passengers on the private charter partied like it was 1999, still more than a decade in the future.

Pat, the boat's owner, was partying onboard that night. He popped by the pilothouse a couple-two-three times, asking, "John, how can you see where you're going?" I couldn't. I just knew where I was. "Sure am glad you're driving tonight!" So was I because Pat couldn't see where he was going, and it had nothing to do with the combination of darkness and fog.

Even as a kid, I was never that bawling lost little boy. After my Grandma Curran boasted to her son, Bill, how I knew my way around despite my age, the following morning, my father, the one responsible for half my DNA, tested his mother's claim, driving me around Elk Creek, trying to get me lost. He didn't tell me there'd be a test, but I didn't need to study because I knew where we were no matter what road he drove.

"Which way?"

"Right."

Checking to ensure I wasn't just giving him directions without knowing our location, he'd ask, "Where will that take us?"

"Swamp Road... then we turn left."

If he didn't drive every country road around Elk Creek before giving up on getting me lost, he came close. Thing was, I'd never been on many of the roads, and even though I could barely see over his pickup's dashboard, I always knew where to go, the GPS in my head telling me where to go, decades before the soothing voice of the GPS Girl would.

It might sound strange, but with the confidence I could "navigate" any situation, I've made what many considered questionable decisions. Like moving to three universities, sight unseen, or the edge of the Empty Quarter, also sight unseen, and then, even though Sue and I had only spent a few days there, to a property off a dead-end dirt road on the side of a mountain in a remote area of southern Ecuador.

Where Sue does the driving because she's much better with a shift stick, and I'm much better at navigating. Sure, we got some looks at first, the not-so-macho man riding shotgun while his wife drove. Together, though, we make a good team, but if we switched roles, with Sue navigating, we wouldn't necessarily get where we're going, and with me manually shifting the gears, with a transmission.

It's why the navigator was the kid in the backseat when Ma, Del, and I went on annual summer driving trips that could cover three to four weeks and three to four thousand miles. While Ma pointed out what looked like nice clean gas stations with a high probability of nice clean restrooms, Del did all the driving. He never steered us wrong because he got good directions from me.

I cemented the navigator's job in the summer of 1974 at the dining room table in stepsister Debbie's apartment in St. Charles, a northwest suburb of St. Louis. Examining a Missouri highway map, the folding paper variety, one we got at a filling station, for free, Ma, Del, and I were trying to determine the best route to Meramec Caverns, a 4.6-mile-long cave system 70 miles to the southwest. Ma suggested, "Why don't we take this blue road?" While it would've gotten us out of St. Charles and headed in the right direction, that blue road was the Missouri River, and Del's Dodge, while a boat, didn't float.

"How about we take I-270 instead."

My favorite navigation memory came three years later - getting us onto the freeway out of downtown New Orleans on our way to Mobile. If you're not familiar with New Orleans, the Mississippi River takes the scenic route through the city, resulting in a street layout that is anything but a rigid grid. To make driving more interesting, nearly every downtown street was one-way. Don't it always seem to go that the easiest way to drive from where you are to where you want to be is down a one-way street… the wrong way?

Sitting in the back seat with a pocket-sized New Orleans street map, the folding paper variety we got from the tourism office, for free, I directed Del to where we wanted to be, Interstate 10 heading east, after an intense minutes-long exchange. We got where we wanted to be without one wrong turn or backtrack, despite the one-way streets and the limited number of on-ramps not marked on the map.

For the 20 or so years I knew Del, he never worried about me, not that I saw. Not because we didn't share any DNA or because he didn't care, but because of experiences like the one we had in New Orleans. After getting him on the on-ramp, he turned and gave me a look, one that showed he believed in me, an unspoken confidence that said, "If you can direct me out of downtown New Orleans reading a pocket map in the back seat of a car bouncing over pothole-filled streets… life better bring it."

034

STORY NIGHT

They were strangers at first, but the more they talked, the more stories they told, the more they became friends, people I knew by name, even if only by their first name. But then I was just a kid, so most adults didn't have last names unless a Mr., Mrs., or Miss preceded it, or in the case of that battle-axe across the street, Old Lady, even if she was only in her thirties.

Like an open mic night at a comedy club, anyone could drop in and share on Friday nights in an old brick building on a corner of Dewey and Wisconsin, just down the street from Eau Claire's largest employer, Uniroyal Tire. Appropriately, the neighborhood was an awkward mix of homes, industrial buildings, and stores between the downtown core and the factory.

Inside the bricks, the décor was '60s cheap. The dark-paneled room was filled with dingy Formica-topped tables surrounded by molded plastic bucket chairs with spindly metal legs. The atmosphere was somber, especially since the lights were always low, as if the storytellers didn't want anyone to see they were there. I got that. When some of my classmates had their turn at show-and-tell, they spent their time talking to their shoes.

They didn't need to dim the lights because, eventually, the cigarette smoke was so thick that I sometimes had a hard time telling the tellers from the listeners. While all that smoke made it hard for me to breathe, cigarettes seemed to help people tell their stories. The good ones knew just when to take a puff to heighten the drama. Besides, if cigarettes were dangerous, the tobacco companies would've put warning labels on their products.

Each week, there was a different host, but no matter who it was, they began with the same question, "Who wants to start us off?" I liked that. Ask for volunteers. I wish my teachers had done the same because maybe the kid in the corner was still working on their story after forgetting to do their homework. Perhaps they just needed to hear others talk first to build some confidence.

If someone didn't want to talk, they didn't have to. I liked that too, thinking it better to have a story told by someone who wanted to tell one than someone forced to. Some never said a word, listening by learning as others told stories. Teachers never let me do that without giving me a low mark for class participation. In my book, listening was participating.

And I liked to listen. A former girlfriend once remarked on how I internalized stories and the storytelling of others, maybe because I got an early start listening to others tell their stories, especially those of big people. With more years behind them, they had more stories to tell, more than a kid like me had anyway. I didn't always understand their stories, but I was interested, if for no other reason than they felt them important enough to share.

One of the best parts about story night was that my Grandpa Curran was one of the storytellers. He was a good one, too. Not just on Friday nights, as he was always telling me something about something, making me a little smarter than I was before. But inside the brick building at the corner of Dewey and Wisconsin, he had a room full of people listening to his words.

I bet they learned a lot because "My Grandpa was smarter than your Grandpa," probably because he read all the time. Before story night, Grandma dropped Grandpa off at the Eau Claire Public Library so he could exchange the stack of books he'd read for another stack he hadn't. Maybe that's why Grandpa had so many stories - because he'd read so many and then went to story night and heard even more.

There were other storytellers, regulars, like my Grandpa. There was Warner, who worked for Northern States Power. He liked story night so much that he came straight from work in the cherry-picker truck he drove for NSP. He spent the day driving around in a truck with a carnival ride. How awesome was that? I don't know how Warner spent his lunch hours, but I know how I would've if I'd been him.

There was Tom, a plumber and a good one, who liked to brag how the police had never arrested him for drunk driving. Grandma shook her head in disgust every time she heard him say that. One night, she decided to do something, lighting a candle for Tom at the Catholic Church she attended in Elk Mound. It worked, too, because that night, Tom was arrested for drunk driving, and he never let Grandma forget how she jinxed him.

Of all the storytellers, other than Grandpa, my favorite was Manley. Tall and thin with silver hair and matching horned-rim glasses, he was a sharp dresser, wearing his Sunday best, even on Friday nights. A smooth talker, I bet he was popular with the ladies, especially when he played basketball for the University of Minnesota in the days before TV. When he'd tell a story with his silky baritone voice, I couldn't help but listen.

And it was primarily men telling the stories. There was a female storyteller every now and then, but most were wives, girlfriends, or other interested parties who came along to listen, like my Grandma. She never told any stories, not at story night anyway, because she was busy behind the counter in the corner preparing sandwiches and setting out cookies and drinks. I helped her because I liked my Grandma. And sandwiches. And cookies, especially if Grandma had baked them - "One cookie for the tray, one for me, one for the tray, one for me…"

As much as I enjoyed story night, I was eager for it to end because everyone got to eat, drink, and tell more stories. With refreshments served, the seriousness of the room faded, and so did the smoke as the storytellers had something else to put in their mouths. After a bite to eat and a sip to drink, they started telling more stories, different ones, happier ones, stories they hadn't shared with the group.

I'd wander from table to table to hear what they said. Maybe because I was the only kid there and they sensed I liked to listen to their stories, everyone was always kind to me. If I had questions, and I always did, they patiently answered them. Some even asked if I had a story to share.

"I punted a ball onto the roof of my school this week!"

"Longfellow? That big one up the hill?"

"Yeah!"

"Well, I think that deserves a cookie! Here, have one of mine."

I learned so much from listening to their stories. I wish I could thank them for sharing, but like Grandpa and Grandma, I doubt any are around anymore - most of them old when I wasn't. Some were young, however. Some were in between. They all had different jobs. Some seemed to have a lot of money, others not so much. Mixed as the buildings in the neighborhood, I didn't understand, then, what they had in common, other than on Friday nights, they gathered in the brick building on the corner of Dewey and Wisconsin to share their stories.

035

THE THINGS I REMEMBER

Bloomer, Wisconsin - Rope Jump Capital of the World! So said the black letters on the white billboard outside town. Nevertheless, for two generations, my Grandpa and Grandma Wall called Bloomer what it was for them - home. Their house at 1208 Oak Street was often a home away from home for me, as it was when I awoke on Christmas morning, seven years old, filled with anticipation of the day to come.

A perfect match for my grandparents, the house was unpretentious. Situated in the first block of homes north of the industrial part of town, six or so concrete steps ended at an open-air front porch notched out of the southwest corner of the house. Wooden half-walls filled in the lengths between columns and the house, but they were topped with boards wide enough that sitting on them was not only possible but almost comfortable, except for that one section in the front that was always loose.

Walking through the front door, the first thing most visitors noticed was a needlepoint in a wooden frame mounted on the wall across from the door. Same as the billboard on the edge of town, only smaller, it too was white with black letters, but instead read "Wall."

"How come only that wall gets a label? What about the other walls? The ceiling? The floor? Maybe that door?"

To the left was the living room. In one corner was a color console TV, and in the other corners, a sectional sofa and a chair big enough to hold three of me. Squeezed between the end of the sofa and the chair was an end table, probably larger than it appeared, but buried in books, newspapers, and magazines, it was hard to see, even with the lamp on top switched on.

To the right was the dining room, with a drop-leaf table. It didn't take up much space when the leaves were dropped but grew considerably when the leaves were raised and then spread, creating room for additional sections, which was necessary when family was home for the holidays. While meant for dining, I played cards - cribbage, 500, hearts, spades, crazy 8s, canasta, go fish, war, solitaire - at that table many more times than I ever ate at it.

In the corner, on a stand, was a smaller black-and-white TV, one mostly only Grandma watched because she could see it from the kitchen. While *Jackie Gleason*, *Hee Haw*, *Wild Kingdom*, *The Wonderful World of Disney*, and Chicago Cubs baseball games aired on the living room TV, game shows, and soaps featured on her TV. I liked the game shows, but when an hourglass filled the screen and the announcer's baritone voice filled the room with the words, "Like sands through the hourglass, so are the days of our lives," that signaled the end of my TV viewing for the afternoon.

In the back right quadrant of the house was that kitchen. Cabinets, fronted by dark brown wood with a hint of red, ran the length of the right wall below the countertop. The cabinets above were interrupted only by a window overlooking the south side yard. The same yard where the family played many contentious games of croquet.

There were steel half-cup pulls on the drawers and the tiniest of metal knobs to open the latches on the doors. In one of the drawers under the countertop was a sheet metal-lined bin where Grandma stored the flour she used to make her delicious pies, cakes, cookies, and bread. Between what steamed on the stovetop, sizzled under the boiler, and baked in the oven, nowhere ever smelled as good as Grandma's kitchen.

Centered on the far end was the door to the enclosed back porch. Along the left wall of the kitchen was the stove and sink, the refrigerator in the back left corner facing the door to the stairs leading to the basement.

At the bottom of those stairs, a door to the left opened to a root cellar with a dirt floor where Grandpa and Grandma stored the "vegetables of their labor" harvested from a garden that almost filled their backyard. A backyard that disappeared from view as the ground sloped down toward an urban creek.

My grandparents' bedroom was tucked away in the back left quadrant of the house. Despite all the time I spent in that house, except to retrieve a winter coat from the massive pile that covered their bed when family was home for the holidays, I could count the number of times I was in their bedroom on one hand and still have a few fingers left over, owing to an unspoken mandate.

The stairs rose from the center of the house to the back between the kitchen and their bedroom. There were three bedrooms upstairs - one overlooking the street and the other two the backyard of the narrow but deep town lot. In each bedroom, there were dormers and sloped ceilings, necessitating even a little guy like me to watch his head. I think it was there the architect in me discovered the best rooms are often those under such roofs, the resulting slopes and angles giving those spaces the interest typical box-shaped rooms lack.

Owing to my good Catholic grandparents and their eight children - six girls and two boys - they needed four bedrooms. They probably would've welcomed an equal number of bathrooms because there was just one on the ground floor between the living room and my grandparents' bedroom. With a toilet, sink, claw-foot tub, and freestanding storage cabinet, there was barely room for one to turn around. I often wondered how they ever managed.

Even though my grandparents' house was "wall-to-wall" with family during the holidays, the lone bathroom was never a problem, owing to another unspoken mandate that no one was to do anything to jeopardize the only working toilet. Oh, but that toilet always made for some drama, as every flush was "I think I can, I think I can, I think I can" slow. Much to everyone's relief, it always could.

Christmas morning or not, as always, no matter how early I got up, Grandpa and Grandma were already sitting at the kitchen table, which made the room feel smaller than it was. Those already up got a head's up to those making their way downstairs, courtesy of a creaky wooden step. The same step that let Grandpa and Grandma know when one (or more) of their children got home from a late night at the Pines Ballroom located a bit further out of town than Bloomer's claim-to-fame billboard.

Grandma usually had a box of Cap'n Crunch around for breakfast when I was. I had to get up early to beat my Uncle Dennis to it or take the chance he'd leave me with Corn Flakes. Then there was Grandma's legendary homemade raisin bread. I had to get up early to get some of that before it was all gone, or I'd be forced to "settle" for Grandma's homemade white bread.

My grandparents' cozy home grew increasingly so that Christmas Day, as family overnighting elsewhere arrived at the house on Oak Street. Lucky me, I was already there, living with Grandpa and Grandma while Ma recovered in the hospital after having her troublesome gallbladder removed.

The night before Christmas, I slept on their living room sofa. Sporting an embossed sort of lazy paisley chocolate brown cover, it was so '60s, but since the year was 1969, it was fitting. The only sofa I'd ever known at Grandpa and Grandma's home, I was disappointed when they exiled it to the basement years later in favor of a new sofa and love seat when I was not around to offer an opinion. While newer, the replacement lacked the character of its predecessor, so I was not disappointed when another sofa set replaced it.

Sleeping on the sofa, not only was I already right where I wanted to be on Christmas morning, but I also had a head start on those slumbering upstairs, even if I wasn't going to beat Grandpa and Grandma to the breakfast table. They were always there first. How did they do that? It might've had something to do with the fact that they went to bed before everyone else. Even me.

Sitting at the kitchen table with my bowl of Cap'n Crunch and a couple of slices of Grandma's raisin bread slathered in real Wisconsin butter, I was anxious for everyone to arrive. Once they did, I'd finally find out what was concealed by the pretty paper that wrapped the packages under the Christmas tree just a few feet from where I'd slept the night before.

"We should open presents… NOW!"

Besides making such profound proclamations, I'm sure I also made a nuisance of myself that Christmas morning. Why, having finished my breakfast and deemed to have no further reason for being there, I was banished from the kitchen. After some protest, I ended up back in the living room on the brown sectional sofa with my knees on the cushions, elbows on the backrest, peering out the side window overlooking the driveway on the north side of the house that led to a seldom-used detached garage in the backyard.

Snow was falling, adding to the already colorless landscape created by previous snowfalls. Through the frost-framed glass, I saw my grandparents' elderly neighbor, Mr. Heitzinger, bundling Mrs. Heitzinger into their car, the driveways straddling the property line. Something didn't seem quite right, but then big people did things I didn't understand then, like why would they drink Leinenkugel's beer when there was a whole case of grape soda chilling on the back porch?

The house quieted after the family finally opened presents and devoured dinner and desserts. So once again, I found myself in the living room on the brown sectional sofa with my knees on the cushions, elbows on the backrest, peering out the side window overlooking the driveways. Mr. Heitzinger returned... but Mrs. Heitzinger... Mrs. Heitzinger did not.

If something wasn't right before, now something was wrong, very wrong, because Grandpa and my Uncle Mike were on either side of Mr. Heitzinger, each with an arm around his back. And Mr. Heitzinger... Mr. Heitzinger looked like a boy who not only didn't get what he wanted for Christmas but also lost everything he had.

For the first time, I realized that sometimes people go away... and they don't come back. Many years later,

Mike told me George was always cheery, right up to that day, but afterward… not so much.

For all the anticipation leading up to the wrapping paper-tearing joy of Christmas, Christmas presents have a way of fading away. Like the brown sectional sofa, the presents that once meant so much outlive their usefulness, replaced by something new. Why I don't recall what presents I got for Christmas that year, or most any year. But every Christmas, I think of Mr. and Mrs. Heitzinger and that snowy December 25th in 1969 because, unlike the presents of Christmas past, these are the things I remember.

036

MISFIT

Oh, The Places You'll Go! Ma presented me with a copy of Dr. Seuss's book in May 1990 after I graduated from the University of Wisconsin-Milwaukee for the third and final time. Little did we know that less than a year later, I'd accept a position to teach computers and math at United Arab Emirates University in the desert oasis of Al Ain on the edge of the Empty Quarter. I'd say Ma nailed the graduation gift.

Always one of the better students, only after moving overseas did I realize how ignorant I was. With 22 years of school and three degrees behind me, the education I thought I'd finally finished had only just begun. Soon realizing I didn't know what I didn't know (unknown unknowns), I kept my eyes and ears open and my mouth shut, mostly, absorbing enough to write a 26-page single-spaced typed letter to family and friends summarizing but a fraction of what I learned my first nine months in the UAE.

Then I returned to Wisconsin for my first summer break and learned one more thing - Thomas Wolfe was right when he said you can't go home again. I got further confirmation each time I returned during my summer breaks. Seeing the States more clearly from the outside, I saw the country I once called home backsliding. When I warned family and friends, most laughed at me, and a few got angry with me. The laughter has since subsided, the growing anger, redirected, mostly.

As awareness of the slippage increased, so did the number of Americans I saw experiencing solastalgia. Solastalgia? After witnessing the devastation caused by strip mines in his home country of Australia, Dr. Glenn Albrecht, a philosopher and former professor at Perth's Murdoch University, coined the term to describe the homesickness one experiences when one is still at home, and home isn't what it used to be.

While the country I knew no longer existed, for better and for worse, the bigger reason I couldn't go home again was because the person I was no longer existed. When I was a student at UWM, a classmate and friend, Craig, told me another friend, leaving for Europe, would not come back… the same person. He explained that they'd never see the world the same after living in another country, even if only for a semester. A change in perspective does that.

Craig, as he often was, was right. My friend did indeed come back a different person than when they left. So you can extrapolate how much I've changed after living over half my life in the UAE, in a culture far different from my own, and in Ecuador, in only a somewhat similar culture. What Craig didn't tell me, but maybe implied, is that after one returns from away or doesn't return, they don't look at their own country the same either. A change in perspective does that, too.

How could my perspective not change after moving to the UAE? Even in 1991, before the boom, Dubai was already on its way to becoming what it is now, one of the world's most cosmopolitan cities, with expats from more than 200 countries speaking more than 140 languages making up 83% of the population. Every year I lived there brought more worldviews with the departure of old expats and the influx of even more new ones.

That turnover hit me particularly hard during my fourth year in the UAE after nearly all my peeps in Al Ain moved back or on. Difficult as it sometimes was, over my last five years in Al Ain, still more friends said goodbye, an unpleasant part of the life I'd chosen, that of a "professional expat." Then came my turn to leave friends behind, including a girlfriend I didn't get back after returning 18 months later.

After six-and-a-half more years of friends saying goodbye, in July 2007, it was my turn again as I moved on, to Ecuador. By then, I'd learned that if I didn't want to lose someone, I should bring them along. As long as they agreed to go, otherwise, the authorities called it human trafficking.

So, as I waited for my last flight out of Dubai to take off, Sue was sitting by my side. After moving from Canada to the UAE in January 2001, she expected to move back, not on to Ecuador with me. I saw such a move coming, though, as I started looking for what we eventually found near Vilcabamba before I first left the UAE and before I met Sue.

Once in Ecuador, even before renovating our home, we began searching for our next stop. Which turned out to be Canada, with our 2017 purchase of a property on Haida Gwaii, a place I'd never heard of until I met Sue. We visited the archipelago in the Canadian province of British Columbia for the first time just before making our first trip to South America, to Ecuador, to buy the property off a dead-end dirt road where I've lived longer than I have at any other locale.

Canada isn't the same for Sue either because she hasn't lived in her home country for over a third of her life. For me, even though Canada's closer to home, literally and figuratively, it's still not home. Because, for reasons I think Canadians understand better than Americans, even Canada isn't just like the United States (but with universal health care, highly regulated banking, sensible gun control, properly funded school systems, and prettier money) and never will be.

"Canada, it's like a whole other country, eh?"

Then, for me, the United States is too. During my first few years as an expat, I grew tired of family and friends asking me when I was moving back as if living in another country could never be as good or rewarding as living in the States. As the years passed, they stopped asking the question, perhaps realizing I was happy and home, wherever I was, and the States, not what it once was, not the country I left.

My Grandpa Curran was not one to ask when I was moving back, instead telling me, more than once, "You have to go where the opportunities are, boy." Little did I know how right Grandpa was because teaching at UAE University turned out to be just one of many opportunities before me as I sat in seat 3A of a United Express jet parked at Gate 1 (there were only two at the time) of the Appleton airport terminal waiting for my expat life to begin. The date? July 27, (Sue's birthday), 1991.

After so many years and counting as an expat, if I could go back and do it over, I would, in a heartbeat. The only thing I'd do differently is to do it sooner if I could. Why? Often feeling like a misfit living in the States, but rarely feeling like one living in countries where I was one, I never felt at home until I left mine.

THE END... OF THIS BOOK

THANK YOU!

Next in the series, **MISFIT 2**, has 36 more stories.

ENJOY!

MISTERJOHN.ME

yakpublishing.com

Printed in the USA
CPSIA information can be obtained
at www.ICGtesting.com
CBHW030737261024
16403CB00043B/573